Italian-America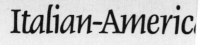

Italian-American Ways

Edited by Fred L. Gardaphe

Bread and biscuit bakers are Loredana, 2, and Adriana, 6, daughters of Mr. and Mrs. Gino Bartucci; Christina Palermo, 78, center; and the girls' grandmother, Maria Carmela Bartucci, 83, in the basement of her Chicago suburban home. Mrs. Palermo and Mrs. Bartucci, lifelong friends, are from the Italian village of Marano Marchesato, Cosenza, Calabria.

PERENNIAL LIBRARY

Harper & Row, Publishers, New York
Grand Rapids, Philadelphia, St. Louis, San Francisco,
London, Singapore, Sydney, Tokyo

FIRST EDITION

LIBRARY OF CONGRESS CATALOG CARD NUMBER 89-45090

ISBN 0-06-096337-9

89 90 91 92 93 FG 10 9 8 7 6 5 4 3 2 1

Contents

4

Introduction

Some of the first immigrants were embarrassed by their past, seeking to forget it. Fortunately the present generation is vitally interested in traditions. As John F. Kennedy once said, "We are a nation of immigrants." We should preserve the heritage and the culture of each of the ethnic groups. Each has contributed to the America we know, and that's what makes America great.   —Anthony Sorrentino

Between 1870 and 1924, twelve million Italians left their native land. Nearly half of them came to America, seeking a new life that would be better than the grinding poverty of southern Italy. Few came after the 1924 change in the United States immigration laws.

Now twenty million Americans claim Italian descent. The third, fourth and fifth generations of Italian Americans retain many of the values and the charm of their grandparents and great-grandparents.

Theirs is a noble heritage. In terms of history, art, architecture, literature, and triumphs of the human soul, the Italian experience has been an inspiration to the western world.

The Italians and the Italian Americans consider family to be of uppermost importance, the core of life and loyalty. From this strength, developed over centuries, came the warmth, hope and love based on the philosophy of the greater family of God, Joseph, Mary, and Jesus. Ninety-five percent of Italian Americans are Roman Catholic.

When one young Italian American from Pennsylvania faced death because of a heart infection in the early 1970s, she had a vision of the Virgin Mary. The Virgin said, "Caterina, you may stay to raise your three children." She lived to raise them.

5

Then, miraculously, in her mid-40s, after bypass surgery to give her heart a few more years, Caterina and her husband welcomed a new baby, Maria, to the world. Will the promise hold? Will Caterina live to raise her new baby? She hopes so, and she and her husband are supremely happy.

One of her children had cancer. Through difficult years in Pennsylvania, the Midwest and on the West Coast, Caterina's faith and her family upheld her. This is the kind of support an Italian American relies on for strength and guidance in times of deep trouble. Knowing that she herself may never grow old, Caterina is a volunteer in a home for the aged.

Despite generational changes, and with many moving from the Little Italies of the cities to the suburbs, Italian-American families remain close. They continue the historic traditions such as Sunday dinners which become treasured feasts of togetherness. Many families gather their generations for weekday meals as well. A second stove to keep the sauces bubbling all day for such large gatherings is a common feature in Italian-American homes. Basements of suburban homes are finished to serve as huge kitchen-dining rooms.

Nowadays, with many Italian Americans marrying outside the ethnic group and with many others becoming more and more a part of mainstream America, the need to preserve the values and uniqueness of being Italian American is greater than ever. Italian Americans need to recognize their contribution to the building of America—the beauty, culture, and enrichment they have brought to family life, faith, politics, business, sports, art, literature, education, and to virtually every phase of life—all this while keeping their roots and heritage always in mind.

The Glowing Ages of Italy

Italy, resembling a tall riding boot thrusting into the Mediterranean Sea, is quickly spotted on a map or globe. The boot and nearby islands of the Italian nation are relatively crowded. Italy has a population of more than fifty-seven million on 116,500 square miles of land.

The distinctive peninsula and its major islands are young in geological terms. The earth's molten interior strained its cooling crust to raise the Apennine mountain range in the age when mammals first appeared. In the most recent million years the Alps were buried under ice that slid slowly down their southern slopes toward the present Po Valley, creating a network of rivers and depositing rich organic matter on the land. These inexorable forces made Northern Italy fertile and its climate continental. It became a basin, a land of lakes, tipping gently toward the Adriatic Sea.

Natural barriers deprived the South of all but a few short, swift rivers that carved out deep gorges and valleys. The South presently lives in the volcanic age, with Etna, Vesuvius, Stromboli and Vulcano still active. The climate is almost tropical, with palms and cacti. Sandy stretches on the Adriatic and rocky headlands in the west offer little opportunity for cultivation, but the people terrace and plow their high, steep land.

Italy's shoreline has always been irresistible to invaders, and its mountains have been barriers to communication between regions, assuring a complex history for this beautiful country.

Although that history traditionally dates from the legendary founding of Rome in 753 B.C., cavemen called "Villanovans" lived on the Italian peninsula 200,000 years earlier.

Greeks and Etruscans came early in the eighth century B.C. The Greeks settled in Sicily, founding independent cities, the most powerful of which was Syracuse. In 456 B.C. Aeschylus, the great dramatist, was killed in Sicily when an eagle dropped a tortoise on his bald head.

The Etruscans, immigrants from the Middle East, settled on the West coast. They were highly civilized. The Etruscans ruled Rome for 300 years, but their power began to fade in the fifth century B.C.

In the *Aeneid,* Virgil (70 B.C.-19 B.C.) wrote of the founding of Rome. He told how a Latin princess who was a virgin priestess in the temple of Vesta, goddess of the hearth and its fires, conceived with the god Mars. Her uncle, the king, was wrathful and abandoned the resulting twin boys on the river bank, where a she-wolf found them and suckled them. When Romulus and Remus grew up, they led a band of rebel youths in search of a new home and chose the site of Rome because a flight of eagles passed over it—a sign from the gods.

Etruscan rule ended in 509 B.C. when the son of a harsh king raped a Roman noblewoman, who then killed herself in shame. This gave Roman noblemen an excuse to revolt, and the Republic was born.

During the next two hundred years, Rome conquered more of the Italian peninsula, but Carthage in North Africa controlled the western Mediterranean. The first clash between Rome and Carthage in 264 B.C. began the Punic Wars that stretched over nearly a century. In the second war, Hannibal and his elephants crossed the Alps into Italy, and in the third war, Carthage was defeated and the ground where it stood was salted to make the soil infertile. The Punic Wars gave Rome Sicily, Sardinia, Spain, and Africa.

Peace meant poverty for many of the common people, but the rulers distracted them with "bread and circuses," distributing bread for sustenance and creating circuses for entertainment.

Julius Caesar was a remarkably able and energetic leader in both war and peace. The empire he built stood for several centuries; its Greco-Roman culture is the basis of modern-day Western civilization. Caesar believed himself divinely appointed to rule Rome. Legend holds that he laughed at a soothsayer's warning to beware the Ides of March, but it was on March 15, 44 B.C. that he was assassinated in the Senate House of Rome. The conspirators included Brutus and others to whom Caesar had extended clemency after defeating them in battle.

Before he achieved full power, Caesar was one of three jointly ruling Rome. Caesar was succeeded by the second triumvirate—his adopted son, grand-nephew and heir, Octavian; his chief deputy and friend, Mark Antony *(Marcus Antonius);* and a military leader, Lepidus. By Caesar's will, Octavian succeeded to the name Caesar. Octavian achieved full power in 31 B.C., beginning the reign of emperors. He became Octavian Caesar Augustus. Augustus is an ancient name suggesting mystical power and superiority over all. As Rome had honored Julius Caesar by changing the name of the month *Quintilis* to July, it honored Caesar Augustus by changing the name of *Sextilis* to August, two calendar changes unchallenged for two thousand years.

Caesar Augustus ushered in the *Pax Romana,* two hundred years of progress and relative peace. Of the emperors who came after Caesar Augustus, only a few are remembered, the good and the terrible. Among the best between A.D. 96 and 180 were Trajan, Hadrian, and Marcus Aurelius. The worst, some of them quite mad, were Tiberius, Caligula, and Nero (who, incidentally, couldn't have fiddled while Rome burned because he was out of town, and the fiddle hadn't been invented yet).

In 395, Constantine divided the empire between East and West. Rome, principal city of the West, was sacked by the Visigoths in 410, beginning four centuries of barbarian invasions. The Dark Ages began with incursions by the Visigoths, then the Ostrogoths and Lombards, who were German tribesmen.

The Church gained more authority in these years. Pope Gregory I persuaded the Lombards to abandon the siege of Rome and sent missionaries to northern Europe. In 726, the pope organized an Italian revolt against the emperor. The Lombards sided with the pope, but he saw a threat in the Lombards and called for help from the Franks, to whom missionaries had been sent. Pepin, king of the Franks, invaded Italy in 754 and gave the lands he conquered to the pope. Twenty years later, his son Charlemagne finished the job and was crowned Holy Roman Emperor in St. Peter's Basilica.

Norman mercenaries arrived in southern Italy in the early eleventh century. Robert Guiscard conquered Calabria, and his nephew Roger conquered Sicily and was crowned king in 1130. Descended from Scandinavians who settled in France in the eighth century, the Normans brought blue-eyed blondness to Sicily.

With the revival of Mediterranean commerce, rich and powerful cities were growing in central and northern Italy. The city-states of Venice, Genoa, and Pisa were known for their fleets. (Today, Pisa is known for its leaning tower.) Milan and Verona had access to Alpine passes. Florence had the Arno river as a route to the sea and controlled two roads to Rome.

Constant fighting in Italy ended early in the fourteenth century, when the popes and emperors withdrew from public affairs. This was the time of the Renaissance, a cultural awakening that even the Black Death could not smother, although the death rate in some cities in 1347 was as high as sixty percent.

City life became violent as families fought each other for power. Merchant princes dominated the government. The most powerful city-state was Milan, where the Visconti family reigned. Florence flourished because of the wool trade and the astuteness of the Medici family.

After the French defeated the Italians at Fornovo in 1495, disruptive foreign intervention began. King Charles V of Spain became Holy Roman Emperor in 1530, and his descendants ruled Italy with an oppressive hand for the next century and a half—a dull period in Italian history.

The harrowing rule of the Austrians followed the Treaty of Utrecht in 1713, but the French Revolution inspired dreams of independence in the people of Italy.

Napoleon invaded Italy in 1796 and was greeted with enthusiasm until it became clear that he was just another oppressor. At least the Kingdom of Italy which he formed acquired a taste for unity, difficult as it was to achieve.

The year 1848 brought revolution all over Europe, and it marked the first Italian war of independence. Giuseppe Garibaldi led the fighting in 1849, later fleeing to New York. From 1852, Count Camillo Cavour led the cause of unity as prime minister of Piedmont. By 1870, Italy was a parliamentary democracy with the king as executive.

The twentieth century found Italy still plagued with the divisions of wealth and poverty. When World War I began, Rome was declared neutral. To bring Italy to their side, the Allies offered Trieste and Trentino, Italian provinces long held by the Austro-Hungarian Empire. Italy agreed, signing a treaty and mobilizing an ill-prepared army.

Postwar inflation and unrest caused factory workers to take to the streets, and the peasants wanted land reform. Italy was ripe for Benito Mussolini; his Fascist party organized in 1919. Mussolini promised to restore the glory of ancient Rome, and in October of 1935 Italian troops headed for Ethiopia, conquerors on the march.

In World War II, more than a million Italian Americans fought for the United States, which sent some of them to do battle in the land of their forefathers, along with other United States troops including Japanese Americans.

Joseph LoCurto of Rochester, New York, recalls that some Italian-American soldiers who saw the beautiful

11

churches, the art, and the vistas of Italy went home to ask, "Mamma, why didn't you tell me about the wonders of Italy?" The answer was that mamma had never seen those wonders; before emigrating, she had never left her village in southern Italy or Sicily.

King Victor Emmanuel III ousted Mussolini in 1943. Imprisoned, Mussolini was freed by German paratroopers, and was placed by Germany at Salò to head a puppet northern Italian government. Sensing failure, Mussolini disguised himself as a German soldier and joined trucks retreating to Innsbruck. With him was his mistress, Claretta Petacci, who had vowed to share his fate. The ruse did not work. He was recognized and captured by Italian Partisans, resistance fighters. On April 28, 1945, he was shot and hung up by his heels for public viewing.

After the war, Italy became a republic. Its colonies were taken away, reparations had to be paid, and the economy was in trouble, but recovery has been achieved. In 1958 Italy became a founding member of the Common Market, and in more recent times, the Craxi government cut inflation. Italy is the fifth largest industrial producer, exceeded only by the United States, Japan, West Germany and France.

Production has not eclipsed aesthetics. Since the Renaissance, at least, Italian style has been avant garde. Italians like to surround themselves with beauty. They want design that is both sophisticated and natural, and have an eye for an essential balance of line, color, and material. Fashion designers like Valentino, Fendi, Ferre, Gianni Versace, Giorgio Armani, Krizia, Missoni, Laura Biagiott, Genny, Salvatore Ferragamo, and Erreuno achieve a special Italian dash in their expression of the eternal feminine mystique.

Italy is the world's third largest producer of silk, and Italian silk ranks higher in quality than that of the Orient. Como in the Lombardy region is the silk center, the source of the fabric for papal vestments and high fashion creations.

Superb design, leather, and workmanship make Italian

shoes special. The big names in that field are Gucci, Ferragamo, Carrano, Beltrami, Magli, and Botticelli.

Fiat bought Alfa Romeo to become Europe's largest producer of automobiles, designing first for a nation that appreciates good lines and speed, and then for the world. The Ferrari automobile has been called the essence of Italian style, combining power and beauty.

Olivetti, known for typewriters, now supplies the world with computers and word processors as well. Memphis furniture is bright-colored and non-traditional in shape, and Alessi cookware is simple, sleek and durable. Tradition continues in blown glass from Murano in Venice, where the art originated in the tenth century, in lace from the Venetian isles, and in Majolica ceramics, named by Dante.

Italian architects have always been good at designing museums, and Gae Aulenti of Milan is still at it. She's the designer of the Palazzo Grassi exhibition space in Venice and the Musée d'Orsay in Paris, and is working on a museum in Barcelona. She has the Italian genius for synthesis that has been at work throughout the glowing ages of Italy.

As we near the end of the twentieth century, Italy has emerged as a most important part of the European and world communities, a respected contributor of material as well as cultural riches.

Christopher Columbus and the Italian Explorers

If Christopher Columbus were to see the Columbus Day parades in New York and Chicago and also see his double coming ashore in the San Francisco re-creation of his landing in the New World on October 12, 1492, he would be totally amazed.

Despite the fact that Watling Island, where he first set foot in the New World, looked nothing like Marco Polo's descriptions of Asia that inspired his voyage, Columbus died believing that he had discovered not a new continent, but a western route to Asia.

Given little recognition in life, Columbus, after his third voyage to the lands of his discovery, was arrested and sent back to Spain in chains.

He deserved honor. Could he return today, he would be gratified to learn that eighteen American cities and towns bear his name, and twenty more are known by a version of it, Columbia; many streets and statues honor him. He would be pleased to discover that the corn, potatoes, cocoa, and tomatoes he brought back from the New World have been returned to these shores to be used by wonderful Italian-American cooks. And he would be simply overwhelmed by the sight of thousands of cheering Italian Americans and others marching each October to honor his memory.

Peter W. Rodino, Jr., who served 40 years as a member of Congress from New Jersey, authored the legislation that made Columbus Day, October 12, a national holiday.

October 12? Just one little day? That won't play in San Francisco. The annual Columbus Day agenda is so crowded that in 1988, for example, the festivities required three full weekends, beginning September 24 with the Queen Isabella

Joseph Cervetto, Sr., lands at San Francisco in a re-creation of the discovery of America by Christopher Columbus.

Pageant featuring 20 contestants. The event was held at Bimbo's 365 Club on—where else?—Columbus Avenue.

The next weekend featured the Queen Isabella Coronation and a three-day Festa Italiana with Italian cuisine, a *bocce* ball tournament, nightly fireworks, puppeteers, magicians, jugglers, a ventriloquist, and guest entertainers.

There was a memorial mass at Fisherman's Wharf Chapel, and the laying of flowers on the bay in memory of those who have perished at sea. Then the New World landing of Columbus was re-enacted by Joseph Cervetto, Sr., assisted by "Queen Isabella," coastal Pomo Indian dancers, and a 45-piece band from Lonate Possiolo, Italy, that performs while running.

On Sunday, there was Solemn High Mass at Saints Peter and Paul Church and the procession of Madonna del Lume, Holy Mother of Light, moving to Fisherman's Wharf for the Blessing of the Fishing Fleet. This 53-year-old San Francisco observance perpetuates a centuries-old religious practice that originated in Porticello, Sicily, honoring Maria del Lume as the *Patrona* of fishermen and their families.

The final weekend of the 1988 celebration included an Old World Festival and Bazaar, Grand Banquet and Ball, Solemn Mass of Commemoration, the 225-unit Columbus Day Parade (on Sunday, October 9) and finally, on Monday, the traditional civic ceremony honoring Columbus, at the Columbus Statue on Telegraph Hill.

Impressive? Actually, everything is mere warmup for 1992. Established by Congress, the Christopher Columbus Quincentenary Jubilee Commission is planning the 1992 American celebration of celebrations on the 500th anniversary of Columbus's discovery.

Born in 1451, Columbus was an apprentice in his father's weaving business until he answered the siren song of the sea in his twenty-fourth year. Legend has it that he came to Portugal by way of a shipwreck, but some historians believe he went to Lisbon to join his brother, a chart-maker, in that great center of navigation.

Correspondence with Paolo Toscanelli, a Florentine humanist and astronomer, helped convince Columbus that the world was round, and he used Toscanelli's letters to support his plea for ships to verify the theory by finding a sea route to Asia.

His negotiations with Ferdinand and Isabella of Spain stretched over six long years. Queen Isabella finally signed the authorization in April 1492, and the rest is history.

Columbus was only one of many Italians who ventured in search of new lands or a westward sea route to the riches of the East. Another Genoa native, Giovanni Cabotto, known as John Cabot, may have been acquainted with Columbus in his boyhood. Cabot, also searching for Asia, discovered Newfoundland in 1497.

Amerigo Vespucci (1454-1512), from a banking family that served the Medici family of Florence, followed a career in exploration and navigating. Moving to Seville, he helped prepare the vessels for Columbus's second and third voyages, and later headed at least two voyages.

Vespucci's voyages were to the West Indies and then southwestward. He named Venezuela ("Little Venice"), discovered the mouth of the Amazon River, and continued much farther south. Columbus thought he had reached Asia. Vespucci was convinced by his own voyages that what he saw was not Asia but a "New World." Vespucci used this term in a letter. Another map-maker, Martin Waldseemüller of Lorraine, read the letter. His next map accepted the "New World" theory and identified the new lands as "America" in honor of the man who recognized them as such, rather than "Columbia," for the one who discovered them.

Giovanni da Verrazzano also tried to reach Asia, sailing under the French flag. The land he reached in 1524, the Atlantic coast of the United States and Canada from the Carolinas to Newfoundland, was named Francesca in honor of King Francis I of France. Nobody remembers that name, but we do remember Rhode Island. The name of the smallest state in the union was inspired by Verrazzano's description of land that reminded him of the Greek island of Rhodes.

Verrazzano sailed into New York harbor. A New York City bridge is named for him, and a bust of him was erected in New York's Battery Park in 1909. Verrazzano also rounded Cape Cod.

Living in America

The Joseph LoCurtos at the Casa. Roman Amphora, a jar 2,000 years old, was gift of the Italian government.

In 1979, Joseph J. LoCurto of Rochester, New York, was named *Cavaliere Ufficiale,* the equivalent of knighthood, by the President of the Italian Republic for contributions to "better cultural relations between our countries." LoCurto conceived and proposed to build a center for Italian studies, choosing Nazareth College of Rochester because of its outstanding language department. He assumed the building committee chairmanship when the 125,000 Italian Americans of Rochester joined hands to build Casa Italiana and to offer scholarships for students studying Italian. Since 1978 the Casa has been a part of the college, with academic and cultural programs, events, concerts, and art exhibits. It is the second of its kind in the United States, after the Casa at Columbia University, which dates from 1914. The Casa at Nazareth and its many supporters stand as a symbol of a new era of service, dignity, and prestige enjoyed by Italian Americans today.

It was not always like this. The rise of the Italian Americans is a story of many years of dedication and effort. Centuries before the high tide of Italian immigration in the years 1870-1924, Italians made their mark on what is now the United States. Explorers led the way.

In 1539, Friar Marco Da Nizza traveled through the Arizona desert to the present site of Phoenix. Venetian glassblowers were invited to join the first permanent settlement at Jamestown, Virginia, founded in 1607, and Venetian beads were in demand for trade with the Indians. The first Italian to live in Brooklyn, then known as New Amsterdam, was Peter Caesar Alberto, who arrived in 1639 and later developed a large tobacco plantation.

Known as "the man with the iron hand," Henri de Tonty arrived in the New World in 1678, built the first sailing vessel to ply the Great Lakes and became right-hand man to the better-known Robert Cavelier, sieur (senior) de La Salle (1643-1687). In 1682, La Salle and Tonty, having explored the length of the Mississippi River, claimed its adjacent lands for France. Tonty also is called the "father of Arkansas" because he established the first European settlement in that state in 1686.

Philip Mazzei came to Virginia in 1773 and found the echo of his revolutionary idealism in Thomas Jefferson. They collaborated on an expression of the principles of the American Constitution, and Mazzei's contribution was the statement, "All men are by nature equally free and independent . . .all men are perfectly equal in natural rights."

Arriving in New Orleans in 1774, Giuseppe Maria Francesco Vigo, a fur trader, impoverished himself in order to finance the conquest of the Northwest Territory. Long afterward, his heirs were compensated for his contribution.

Alessandro Malaspina served the young nation by leading a 1791 scientific expedition that surveyed the Pacific coast from Alaska to Mexico.

The Coronado and De Soto expeditions in the 1540s included Italians—the first to arrive in what is now Texas. In the battle of San Jacinto, which won Texas its independence from Mexico in 1836, there was an Italian on each side—Vincente Filisola, second in command to Santa Anna, and Prospero Bernardi, a volunteer in the Texas forces.

Antonio Meucci, who came to Cuba in 1835, accidentally discovered the principle of the telephone while experimenting with electricity. He moved to New York in 1850 to be closer to a source of technical equipment. His discovery was well in advance of Alexander Graham Bell's recognition of the same principle in 1874.

In the same year Giuseppe Garibaldi, leader of the Thousand Redshirts in the Italian national revival, arrived in New York as a political refugee. Meucci invited Garibaldi to live with him. For a time, the two survived on fish and game and the meager profits from making candles, before Garibaldi returned to his guerrilla wars which made the Italian nation possible. The house they shared is now the Garibaldi Meucci Museum of the Order Sons of Italy in America, at 420 Tompkins Avenue, Staten Island, New York. The museum celebrated its 100th anniversary in 1989.

Garibaldi's dream, the unification of Italy, would come to pass, but it would be a mixed blessing. The more prosperous North wanted military development, which led to conscription and heavy taxes for the impoverished South. By 1870 Italian immigration had increased dramatically. Unlike the earlier immigrants, many now came expecting to prosper in America and go back home. Accustomed to living out their lives within the sound of the bell from the campanile of their birthplace, they joined earlier Italian immigrants for help and moral support. People from the same village would settle in the same American neighborhood, relying on those who had arrived earlier to find jobs for them. The experienced immigrants who knew the ropes were called *padroni*.

If life was hard at home, it was no better in America, and sometimes it was worse, but still they came. They arrived with nothing, and they were ill-paid for their hard labor. Until immigrant protection societies were established, only their resilient nature kept the Italians from total despair.

New York and particularly Brooklyn attracted the most Italian immigrants. Italians are still one of the largest ethnic groups in all of New York City with a concentration on Mulberry Bend in Little Italy on the lower east side.

After 1880 Hartford, Connecticut began to attract about five thousand Italian immigrants each year, and they settled in the Little Italy area around Front Street and Windsor Avenue. Among them were the Loraias, founders of the largest Italian commercial bank in New England.

Boston's north end drew many ethnic groups late in the nineteenth century, but by the 1920s the area was almost entirely Italian. The celebration of the Feast of Saint Anthony in late August now seems like native custom in former Puritan territory. Providence, Rhode Island claims a twenty percent Italian-American population, and the Federal Hill neighborhood, especially Atwells Avenue, is a paradise for diners and food shoppers.

Philadelphia, which saw its first northern Italians in 1853, later became a way station for southern Italians en route to the Pennsylvania coal mines. South Philadelphia boasts a quarter of a million Italian Americans and a wonderful open-air fruit and produce market on Ninth Street. Folklorists are finding Philadelphia a rich mine of Italian folk arts, including palm weaving. Palms are woven and sold at Easter time and as grave decorations.

Especially on the East Coast, Italian-American bread sculptors, needlework artists, stone carvers, and the creators of vast Christmas crèches flourish. Many of the stone carvers in Barre, Vermont, came from Carrara, Italy.

In Baltimore, the Italian district around High and Fawn streets is known simply as "The Neighborhood" and it's rich in Italian restaurants.

New Orleans attracted the Sicilians. They had a reputation for being ambitious and hard-working, prompting Louisiana to form an Immigration League to lure them to the state. They settled in the French Quarter and soon had their own Little Palermo, moving quickly into the merchant ranks of the city.

In 1985 the American Italian Museum opened next to the award-winning Piazza d'Italia in downtown New Orleans.

Financed by the Italian-American community, the museum contains art works, the Diamond Jim Moran exhibit with mink neckties, a St. Joseph's Altar replica, opera singer Marguerite Piazza's Mardi Gras ball gown, and other mementos. The papers of Giovanni Schiavo, an authority on Italian-American history, and immigrant family histories are in the library.

The first Italians to settle in St. Louis arrived after 1850 and more new arrivals came in a steady stream well into the twentieth century. The district known as "the hill" is noted for Italian neighborhood shops and restaurants.

California beckoned to the northern Italians. Before the 1906 earthquake brought business to a grinding halt, A. P. Giannini, founder of the Bank of America, had removed the assets of his small Italian savings and loan society elsewhere. While the fires still burned, he came back to finance the rebuilding of the city.

Andrea Sbarboro (Italian Swiss Colony) and the Gallo brothers became California wine barons. Marco Fonatana's California Fruit Packing Corporation grew to be the largest operation of its kind in the world.

San Francisco's North Beach is home to many Italians. They came during the Gold Rush, hoping to strike it rich and go home to northern Italy in style. Some did just that, but others stayed to farm in the fertile valleys, supply the seafood at Fisherman's Wharf, engage in banking, and support the opera. Their combined influence has made Columbus Day into San Francisco's Mardi Gras.

More than a half-million Italian Americans served in the United States Armed Forces during World War II. They were in all branches of the service, including the divisions that drove the Germans out of Italy. Twelve Italian Americans were awarded the Congressional Medal of Honor. The Navy named destroyers for two of these—Corporal Anthony Damato of Shenandoah, Pennsylvania, and Marine Sergeant John Basilone of Raritan, New Jersey.

Census figures show that New York state ranks first in Italian population; the Dakotas are last. New York City tops the list of fifteen cities with the largest Italian population, followed by Philadelphia, Chicago, Boston, Los Angeles, Pittsburgh, Detroit, San Francisco, Providence, Buffalo, Cleveland, Washington, D.C., Rochester, Fort Lauderdale, and New Haven, Connecticut. Communities of Italian Americans are found in Tampa, Florida and Galveston, Texas, where fishing is important, and in many other cities.

Today, Italian-American debutantes make their bow to society at the Italian Heritage Ball and Cotillion in Chicago, at two cotillions in Cleveland, and at *Ballo di Natale* every December in New Orleans. Founders of the first ball in Cleveland were Stella Zanoni and Sue Gallucci. Italian-American organizations sponsor the balls. Ann Sorrentino, first chairperson of the Chicago Cotillion, says, "It's a mark of success to be able to present a daughter at such a lovely and prestigious occasion." It's also a long way from the immigrant struggle.

The founder of the National Italian American Foundation, Jeno Paulucci, is from Virginia, Minnesota, an Iron Range town. He succeeded so well in business (canned and prepared Chinese foods, and Jeno's Pizza) that he can practice philanthropy without stint.

The University of Minnesota boasts the Immigration History Research Center in St. Paul, founded in 1965 and directed by Rudolph Vecoli, whose doctoral dissertation was about the Italians in Chicago before World War I. Early Italian newspapers and manuscripts by Italian writers are a part of the collection. With John Andreozzi, project coordinator, the Order Sons of Italy in America has sponsored a project to gather its archives. Efforts like these help to fill the gaps in the thinking of Italian Americans—the gaps between the hardships of ocean voyages in steerage to reach a new land, and the comparative luxury of the debutante cotillions of today.

Growing Up Italian in America

by Fred L. Gardaphe

Growing up in an Italian family is marked in two ways. There are the informal stages, noted by table placement during family meals: the little children sit together at their own table near the adults. Then there are the formal stages which are usually religious, marked by baptism, First Holy Communion, confirmation, marriage and, finally, the funeral.

So much of our heritage revolves around the gathering, preparing and consuming of food that being Italian is often equated with eating well. I used to think that the only thing outsiders knew of Italians was their food. This bothered me until I realized that our ancestors were immigrants whose lives in the "old country" were centered around the production of food for survival. Perhaps that's why most third-generation Italian Americans, when asked what being Italian means to them, respond with a reference to their large family meals.

In addition to being celebrated on festive occasions, the meal attended by the extended family of generations of brothers, sisters, and cousins is at least a once-a-week ritual, usually held at the home of the grandparents.

The Sunday Dinner

The front door of my grandparents' apartment was always left open on Sundays. The hallway smelled of a mixture of freshly waxed woodwork and garlic frying in olive oil. I'd head straight for the kitchen where Grandma would be standing in front of the stove, turning cloves of fresh garlic in a pool of sizzling oil. After kissing her I'd head to the back porch, the site of Grandpa's workshop, where he would make his sausage. Grandpa would usually be out in the back yard, gathering the fresh spices and vegetables that would be used

24

in the day's meal. I'd greet Grandpa from the upstairs window and then join him in the garden. I'd do this more to get out of the kitchen than for any love I had for gardening, because gardening was hard work.

Men would never take a seat in the kitchen on Sunday afternoons. That was the women's sanctuary, ruled by Grandma, tended to by my many aunts and invaded only by the most daring of my uncles. Often I'd lean into the kitchen to watch the preparations. I can see it now. . .

The stove begins to sing the stages of the meal. Peppers and onions are popping in the hot oil of the black pan. The sauce gurgles as it sucks in the ingredients that Grandma throws in with her left hand and stirs with her right. She never measures the pepper, salt, or oregano. She doesn't even look to see if she is grabbing the right ingredients. She just dips her hand into the brown bags of spices that sit on a small enamel-covered table next to the stove. If she ever went blind she could probably continue to cook with no change in the taste of her meals.

Grandma leaves the wooden spoon in the sauce to grab the sausage. She drops the links into the large frying pan and turns the heat under the sauce higher. She makes the sign of the cross and looks up to the picture of the Madonna that hangs over the stove. The glass over the picture is spotted with drops of oil and red sauce.

As the rest of the family arrives the groups separate. After a brief stop in the kitchen to greet Grandma, the men head for the living room where they sit, smoke, and talk about the week's events. The children head for the back porch to play with the same wooden blocks, tin soldiers, and rag dolls their parents used years earlier. Grandma never throws anything out.

Directed by Grandma, the women move into action. They lay padding on the large oak table, smooth out the lace tablecloth, and place piles of flower-decorated plates and silverware on top. They scurry in and out of the kitchen, wearing flowered aprons that were once presents to Grandma. All are spotted with red stains of spaghetti sauce, and are in various stages of wear.

One aunt is in the bedroom that opens out into the living room, preparing the card table for the children. Others are placing huge wooden salad bowls, salt and pepper shakers, decanters of Grandpa's wine, small bowls of oil, salt and pepper for dipping *finocchio,* and platters of bread onto the already overcrowded table where the adults will eat.

Being the oldest, I am the errand boy sent into the women's world to fetch beers and bottles of wine. I return to the kitchen to see the stovetop covered with steam that pours out from the two large pots cooking more than five pounds of pasta. I peek into the pot of sauce. The heavier neckbones and sausages have sunk to the bottom and meatballs bob on the surface. Uncle Carmen sneaks in behind me and dips his finger into the boiling red, plucking a meatball with his thumb and forefinger. He then stuffs the whole meatball into his mouth and walks back into the living room. His white shirt holds the drops of sauce that escaped his tongue. I try the same, but as my hand reaches the rim of the same pot Grandma emerges from the pantry, bouncing a colander against my head. "Don't be a *porco.* We gonna eat now. The pasta she ready."

"Ay!" calls an uncle. "Where's my beer?"

"No more beer. *Mangiamo. Mangia, Mangia!"* Grandma sings and chairs scrape the floor and feet shuffle to the tables.

At the head of the table to the far left sits Grandpa. His face is in a full grin and both elbows rest on the table with his hands clasped for prayer. On either side of Grandpa is an uncle, next to him his wife, and so on around the table. All the men wear white short-sleeved shirts, dark ties loose around opened collars. The aunts wear printed cotton dresses, still covered by the aprons. There is one empty chair at the other end of the table. Grandma will sit there.

In the center of the table are platters of neckbones, meat-balls and sausages that have been scooped from the sauce. On either end of the table sit bowls filled with red sauce. A red mist rises from these dishes, thick enough to tingle your nostrils.

The children's table is filled with dishes and silverware, empty of food except for a platter of sliced homemade bread. Their plates will be filled from the bowls and platters on the grownups' table. Grandma enters the room and all heads turn in her direction. She holds a huge platter of the cooked spaghetti. The large pile hides her face. She places the pasta in front of Grandpa and takes her seat. Conversation stops. All eyes are on Grandpa.

Grandpa sniffs the pasta, bows his head toward folded hands and begins the prayer. He always says it in Italian, but the rest mumble it in English. Grandpa makes the sign of the cross and starts to fill the plates. He fills each one with what *he* thinks a person should eat. When all the plates are filled, the sauce is passed around (for years we referred to spaghetti sauce as "gravy," perhaps because we rarely, if ever, would eat meat with thick gravies). Plates of meat follow and all the formalities are finished. The talk resumes and gets louder. The clatter of silver against china creates a din that has to be yelled over.

The meal lasts forever and when it's over the men retire to the living room to resume pre-dinner conversation; some drop off into bedrooms to sleep off the meal. The women clear the tables and return to their sanctuary to preserve the leftovers and wash the dishes. The children head for the back yard, for their energy is not diminished by the meal; they know well that any disruption of the men's rest or the women's work will result in verbal and sometimes physical reprimands.

The whole family stays at Grandpa and Grandma's home through early evening to catch up on each other's lives, discuss common work projects such as home or business improvements, and plan upcoming celebrations.

On the Outside

Southern Italians are typically wary of outsiders, a caution that has its roots in the centuries of invasions the Italians endured. This leads to a complex set of rules for public behavior and a scale of respect: first the family, then the neighbors, finally the officials. In this order is the allegiance of traditional Italian Americans. One's public behavior is closely monitored, and any violations are reported. I can remember walking a girl home from school, then kissing her when we parted ways. By the time I arrived home my mother had received a phone call from a neighbor warning her about my behavior. I was reprimanded and from then on I checked for observers before trying something like that. (In high school, my generation of the 1960s called Italian-American girls "the untouchables.")

School and Work

Priorities of the Italian family are work and one's contribution to the family's well-being. Early on, children are taught that work is important and that providing for the family's survival is more important than individual rewards. Whether it means working in the home or outside in the family business, Italian-American children are expected to obey their elders and contribute as much as possible to the family. Paychecks of children who live at home are quite often not personal property. For many, payday means handing the check over to Mamma, who doles it out as she sees fit.

Though the traditional lack of trust in formal education has weakened considerably over the generations, Italian-Americans are still below the national average in years of education, despite being above the national average in terms of income. This imbalance will undoubtedly disappear in the next generation, but it does point to a peasant-based peculiarity about the role of education in the family's survival.

Going off to college means leaving the family, and once was frowned upon, especially if the family had developed a successful business. Even today, Italian-American children who go into professions are expected to work in the family business if there is one. One doctor and his wife have lived world-wide, but when they visit her family they are expected to do whatever is necessary in the family catering business—wash dishes, stuff olives, et cetera. "If the family is short-handed, you pitch in."

Quite often there are tensions between what is best for the family and what will advance individual career goals. Moving outside the neighborhood, let alone to another state, for a job promotion can create a crisis for the family. If a family is able to stay in the same city, brothers and sisters often buy homes close to one another on the same suburban street, which encourages easy gathering for weekday and Sunday meals.

"Chi lascia la via vecchia per la nuova, sa quella che lascia ma non sa quella che trova" is an Italian proverb that tells us, "He who leaves the old way for the new knows what he leaves, but not what he will find."

Although traditional Italian-American ways, once life-long rules, are no longer adhered to exactly as they were in the past, they are nevertheless still remembered by third-generation family members and will continue to appear in various forms as long as there is an Italian-American identity.

The present generation may speak the language of the adopted land, but certain core values of the immigrants, such as respect for others, the importance of family, and neighborhood concern, continue to survive.

Family Celebrations

by Fred L. Gardaphe

The names that parents give to their children are very important to Italian Americans. One tradition is to name the first-born male after the father's father; the first-born female after the father's mother; the second-born male after the mother's father; and the second-born female after the mother's mother.

Once this process has been fulfilled, families with more than four children reach out to favorite saints for other names. This process often leads to a great number of children bearing the same names in a large family. That's where nicknames become vital in separating identities.

The role of the baptism, though a religious formality, takes on extreme social importance in Italian-American families. The choice of godparents is labored over for hours, even days, by parents and grandparents. Usually those chosen are from outside the immediate family circle. It is an honor that often cements a non-blood relationship. Middle names of children usually come from their godparents. Godparents play an active role in the lives of their godchildren. They become the child's protector and adviser, and sometimes serve as intermediaries between the child and parents.

Elaborate outfits of satin and lace are created soon after the child is born, usually by the seamstress of the family, often the same woman who produced the wedding dress. The day of the baptism is treated much as is a wedding. Family and friends meet at the church to witness the event. Gifts of money are presented to the parents by the guests, and the parents give gifts to the godparents.

Saint's Day

Take a look at a Catholic calendar and for each and every day you will see written the name of a saint. Just as important as a birthday is one's saint's day—the saint who is honored on the day the child was born or the saint whose name the child shares. On these days relatives come to the home of the honoree and present him or her with a small gift. Guests are welcomed to a prepared family meal.

First Holy Communion

The age of seven, according to the Catholic Church, begins the child's ability to reason and thus to be responsible for his or her actions. This is the age of the first Holy Communion, when the child first receives the host—the Body of Christ. Children prepare for this event by studying religious lessons. One's first communion is an important occasion to Italian Americans. The girls dress up in white dresses, similar to short bridal gowns. The boys are usually fitted with their first suit. Friends and family attend the event, which is followed by a large celebration to which guests bring monetary gifts.

Confirmation

A sacrament in the Catholic Church, confirmation is also a way of telling the world that you are old enough to take on more adult responsibilities, such as being able to begin work. Among Italian Americans a confirmed person takes on a third godparent: a male for the boys and a female for the girls. Accompanying the event is the taking of a third name, either a child's favorite saint or often the name of the godparent. The event includes a festive celebration at the family's home, and guests present gifts of money.

The Wedding

Traditionally, Italian-American children are expected to live with the family until they marry, and sometimes even then to remain with the family until they can afford their own home. Going off to college has changed this tradition, but even after college graduation many Italian Americans return to live with the family. An unmarried son or daughter may continue to live with the parents for life.

Marriage is perhaps the most important event for the Italian-American family. It signifies the continuation of the family pattern, expands the network of friends and relatives, and strengthens the family bond. "A new marriage is like a new birth," says an Italian proverb.

Italian Americans are no longer marrying solely inside their ethnic group. Sociologist Richard Alba found in a study that seventy-two percent of Italian-American men and sixty percent of the women marry outside their ethnic group. As a result, seventy percent of Italian Americans born after 1970 have been children of intermarriages. Nevertheless, the wedding still carries many elements of the traditional Italian celebration. The typical event takes place inside a Catholic Church. The reception, once held in the home, is now held in fraternal organization or banquet halls. Home cooking has been replaced by elaborate catering.

Upon arrival at the reception a guest greets each member of the family with a hug and a kiss. In earlier days, the bridegroom and the father of the bride would stand at one table and pour shots of liquor for the male guests; the bride and her mother would stand behind an adjacent table and pour glasses of sweet liqueurs such as *rosolio* for the women guests. The bride carried a satin bag, called *la borsa,* into which the envelopes containing monetary gifts, called *le buste,* were placed.

Years ago a wedding was an event for the entire family, attended by even the smallest of children. This often meant that one hundred invitations could bring five or six hundred people. The guest list is extremely important. At one wedding there were 1,000 invited guests, but the bridegroom forgot two business acquaintances who have not spoken to him since.

Early Italian-American weddings were called "peanut weddings" or "football weddings"—the former because bushels of peanuts were served, the latter because wrapped sandwiches would be passed to the guests. Yet even the earliest of Italian-American weddings were elaborate affairs. Sweets tables filled with homemade cookies, *cannoli,* and a variety of pastries could stretch ten to fifteen yards.

A custom with a long history calls for the table's centerpiece to be a huge tiered cake, often with a pair of love birds placed inside a hollow layer so that when the cake is cut, the birds fly out. At one wedding, the cake was baked in sections to fit onto a carpenter-built framework through which the couple walked and released the white doves.

The cost of an Italian wedding today may rival the price of a small house in the suburbs. Sometimes houses are mortgaged to pay for the wedding, but it also is not unusual for the monetary wedding gifts to equal the cost of the wedding. Showers for the bride often furnish the house or apartment for the young couple.

Weddings are meant for dancing and music, traditionally created by a mandolin and an accordion, moving from lullabies to fast-paced *tarantelle.* Usually a family member joins the band and sings traditional songs such as *C'è la luna* or *Che sarà, sarà.* The celebration lasts long into the night, and may continue even after the bride and groom are gone.

The typical Italian-American wedding is a once-in-a-lifetime event; divorce is rare.

Funerals

Italians are not people who hide their emotions. So when someone dies, especially suddenly or at a young age, grief is unharnessed. One of my earliest memories is of a woman screaming in Italian and throwing herself into the grave as they lowered her husband's coffin. The undertaker and pallbearers all scrambled to pull her out and carry her off. One of my most haunting memories is of the day my father was killed and I headed home. Our house was filled with all our relatives. All the women had gathered on the front porch and were screaming and moaning a collective grief.

Giuseppe Savino, left, of Chicago, watches a grandchild while his wife, Caterina, wearing black, greets a friend at a festa in Berwyn, Illinois. The Savinos are from Italy. Mrs. Savino, whose brother died, will wear black for eight years in his memory.

Food is an important part of this final celebration of life. The family of the deceased does not cook, so friends and relatives bring food already prepared.

Holy cards are printed with scenes of saints and sacred icons on the front and pictures of the deceased on back. This comes from an Italian tradition of pasting posters on village walls announcing someone's death.

The Italians continue to honor and remember their dead with regular visits to the cemetery, and some hold elaborate picnics at the gravesites. My father is buried in a mausoleum and we still bring food when we visit there.

Death means wearing black. In the past, close relatives of the deceased wore black for months, even years after the funeral. Widows were expected to wear black at least until they remarried. Even the children would wear black. Except in isolated instances, this custom is not generally observed today.

Sainthood in America

A frail little girl from Lombardy who became a saint is responsible for the continuing work of healing at three major American medical centers. She is venerated as Saint Francesca Xavier Cabrini, and her memory is celebrated on November 13.

She named the hospitals she founded "Columbus" for the great explorer. Today they bear her own name: Cabrini Medical Center and Cabrini Hospice at 227 East 19th Street, New York City; Columbus-Cabrini Medical Center with hospitals at 2520 North Lakeview Avenue and 811 South Lytle in Chicago; and St. Cabrini Hospital at 920 Terry Avenue in Seattle.

Maria Francesca Cabrini was born in Sant'Angelo on July 15, 1850. As a small child, she dreamed of being a missionary. Her resolve did not waver, even though she nearly drowned trying to sail paper boats to the unsaved of China, each boat carrying violets representing nuns.

At eighteen, she was refused entry to the convent of the Daughters of the Sacred Heart because of her delicate health, but she soon became the substitute for a sick schoolteacher in Vidardo—a task that went on for two years.

When her parish priest became a monsignor in Codogno, he asked her to take charge of an orphanage there, and the pattern of her life began to show its lovely colors. She became Mother Cabrini, superior of the House of Providence, in September 1877. With her religious vows, she added the name of the great missionary, Saint Francis Xavier, to her own.

By 1887, she had founded seven houses of the Missionary Sisters of the Sacred Heart, and then she went to Rome, where she established a free school and a boarding school.

Bishop Giovanni Scalabrini, who founded the Congregation of Saint Charles Borromeo to help immigrants in America, asked Mother Cabrini to go to New York and help the Italian orphans there.

With the blessing of Pope Leo XIII, she and several others embarked for America in 1889. No one met them, and soon they knew why. A letter written by Archbishop Corrigan, telling them not to come because they were not needed, was sent too late.

Undaunted, Mother Cabrini opened a small school for Italian children in the church of Saint Joachim. She saw such wretched conditions among the immigrants that she pressed for an orphanage, and the first of many opened on April 21, 1889.

The Missionary Sisters of the Sacred Heart were on the move, carrying their efforts to Brooklyn, and to Newark, New Jersey. They acquired West Park, a large property on the Hudson sold by the Jesuits because no well-water had been found. Mother Cabrini had a dream that led the well-digger to the site of a natural spring.

The order moved on to found schools and orphanages in France, Spain, England, and Latin America. Mother Cabrini was in Rome when she learned of the New Orleans lynching of eleven Italians following their acquittal in a trial for the murder of an assistant police chief named Hennessey. She went to Nicaragua to establish a school and then to New Orleans in the spring of 1892 to uplift the Italians still suffering from the atrocity of the lynching.

The Missionary Sisters of the Sacred Heart ministered to workers on the docks of New Orleans and visited hospitals and prisons. Mother Cabrini was sensitive to the needs of Italian prisoners and did all she could to brighten their days, even visiting them herself. There is a Mother Cabrini statue in New Orleans on public property.

After Bishop Scalabrini's New York hospital went bankrupt, Mother Cabrini opened Columbus Hospital in 1892. It took in typhoid patients from an Italian merchant ship, and gained support for a new facility that opened in 1895.

Continuing her work with schools and orphanages in Argentina, France, and Brazil, Mother Cabrini was summoned to Chicago in 1899 to found a school. Anemic and wracked with recurring malaria, she never faltered in her labors.

She established a school in England and a college and an orphanage in Spain before going to Denver in 1902 to found a school. In Colorado, she and her nuns went down into the mines to bring the love of Christ to the miners.

A year later, she took over Chicago's North Shore Hotel for a hospital and went to Seattle to start a parochial school and orphanage. She became an American citizen in Seattle.

Chicago's Columbus Hospital opened in 1905 in Lincoln Park. Columbus Extension Hospital was opened in 1910 to serve Italian immigrants on Chicago's west side. It was later renamed Saint Cabrini Hospital. Mother Cabrini thought she was dying in 1912, but she was spared to found a school and orphanage in Philadelphia that year and a hospital in Seattle in 1915.

Cabrini College in Radnor, Pennsylvania honors Mother Cabrini's memory. It is coeducational, and has more than 1,000 students. Mother Cabrini High School in New York City and Cabrini High School in New Orleans are also tributes to her memory.

Mother Francesca Xavier Cabrini died in Chicago December 22, 1917, at the age of 67. She was buried at West Park in New York City.

Investigations concerning her sanctity began in 1928. Medical authorities confirmed cures of hopeless afflictions resulting from prayers to Mother Francesca Xavier Cabrini. Her beatification in the Vatican Basilica took place November 13, 1938, and the full celebration of her sainthood in St. Peter's was on July 7, 1946. Bells of the four hundred churches of Rome lauded America's immigrant saint, and countless Americans of every ethnic descent still bless her name.

High in the mountains near Golden, at a site overlooking Denver far below, is a shrine of the Missionary Sisters of the Sacred Heart, honoring their founder, Mother Cabrini. In *Fra Noi,* the Chicago area Italian newspaper, Ed Marolla describes the approach to the shrine as "similar to the roads of northern Italy, criss-crossing the face of the mountain."

In the convent there is a small bed, a pair of shoes, and other items belonging to Mother Cabrini. Marolla wrote:

"The bed was made of iron, typical of the period, but evidently built for a child—an adult could hardly have lain in it. Yet this was Mother Cabrini's bed, and now we understood why she is so often referred to as the 'little nun.'"

Steps to the shrine were cut by Italian-American miners, stonecutters and sculptors. On either side are Stations of the Cross and the fifteen Mysteries of the Rosary, finely sculptured of stone. At the top of the mountain is a twenty-two-foot statue of the Sacred Heart on an eleven-foot base. The rugged miners and skilled craftsmen contributed their talents and energy to the shrine in memory of Mother Cabrini.

A Pioneer Priest

From a Milanese *palazzo* to a miner's cabin in Benton, Wisconsin, is a great distance today, and in the nineteenth-century lifetime of Father Samuel Mazzuchelli, it was even farther.

Born November 4, 1806, the seventeenth child of a Milan banker who lived near the *Piazza del Duomo,* Carlo Gaetano Samuele Mazzuchelli was a pious boy who studied in Switzerland and later attended the Dominican House of Studies in Rome.

He was persuaded to cross the sea to serve the vast area of the Great Lakes country and upper Mississippi River basin, where no priest had ministered for a century. He arrived in America in 1828. After more study in the new land, he was ordained in Cincinnati in 1830 and began his work in the parish of Detroit, which at that time was an area larger than his native country. He ministered to the Indians and to French traders and settlers for fourteen years, traveling by snowshoe, canoe, and horseback.

Father Mazzuchelli built at least twenty-five churches, laying the stones with his own hands. The first, St. John at Green Bay, Wisconsin, was erected in 1831. St. Mathias, in Muscatine, Iowa was partially constructed up-river in 1842, and was rafted down the Mississippi. Father Mazzuchelli founded eight schools, including two at Sinsinawa Mound, Wisconsin, where he established the Dominican Sisterhood.

Father Mazzuchelli died of pleuro-pneumonia on February 23, 1864. Mourners collected jars of soil from his grave the day he was buried, and today many visit the gravesite at Benton, Wisconsin with reverence.

On July 9, 1964, Mother Benedicta of the Sinsinawa Dominican Sisters formally petitioned for the beginning of the investigation leading to his beatification. The necessary tribunal for the process was named on September 14, 1966. The road to sainthood is much longer when the cause is taken up long after the candidate's death, because there are no living witnesses to sanctity.

Anne B. Short of the University of Wisconsin, Madison, has written a booklet *Reflections Along the Mazzuchelli Trail* to be used as a guide for a day's tour from Madison through Mazzuchelli country.

Ed Marolla, son of an Italian immigrant miner and publisher of the *Horicon (Wisconsin) Reporter*, writes, "Father Mazzuchelli was part of that great vanguard of Italian-American pioneers who led the way for the millions of Italian immigrants. Mazzuchelli country is the one true national Italian American historical shrine."

"Mazzuchelli country," Sinsinawa Mound and Benton are in the southwest corner of Wisconsin, across the Mississippi river from Dubuque, Iowa.

'I Have Had to Suffer'

This is what I say: I would not wish to a dog or to a snake, to the lowest and most unfortunate creature of the earth—I would not wish to any of them what I have had to suffer for things that I am not guilty of. But my conviction is that I have suffered for things that I am guilty of: I am suffering because I am a radical, and indeed I am a radical; I have suffered because I am an Italian, and indeed I am an Italian; I have suffered more for my family and for my beloved than for myself; but I am so convinced that I am right that if you could execute me two times, and if I could be reborn two other times, I would live again to do exactly what I have done.

—*Bartolomeo Vanzetti*

Nicola Sacco, a shoemaker, and Bartolomeo Vanzetti, a fish peddler, were convicted of a 1920 armed robbery and murder in Massachusetts. They were executed August 23, 1927. Fifty years later Massachusetts Governor Michael Dukakis declared August 23 to be Sacco and Vanzetti Day, in memory of the two who he said had been put to death without a fair trial.

Italian-American Organizations

Italian immigrants faced many barriers in the new land. They came without knowing the language, and with different notions about government. Without a familiar church, without representatives in government, and knowing that they had to survive in this country, they turned to each other for support. So began the long tradition of the Italian-American organizations.

Because so many immigrants arrived without families, the earliest organizations consisted of men who banded together outside the work place to aid each other, and were called *Societa di Mutuo Soccorso*—literally, society of mutual support.

Founded in 1905, the Order Sons of Italy in America is the oldest and largest organization of Italian Americans, with 22 chapters and 390,000 members in the United States and Canada. Goals include preserving and disseminating the cultural heritage of Italy and promoting the positive image of Italian Americans in the United States. The national headquarters are in Washington, D.C.

As "Little Italies" gave way to urban renewal and to second- and third-generation moves to the suburbs, Italian Americans organized neighborhood clubs with the purpose of preserving the integrity of their neighborhoods. Regional clubs and clubs for villages and cities were formed to preserve identity and local traditions.

Each small town in Italy has its patron saint, and the honoring of the saint continues through the efforts of the many saints clubs which organize local *feste*.

Italian Americans, now making up nearly twenty-five percent of Catholics in this country, have a strong presence in religious organizations such as the Knights of Columbus.

As soon as the family was economically stable, Italian Americans turned their hearts and pocketbooks to charitable endeavors. One of the earliest of these organizations was Amerital UNICO, founded in 1922. With a membership today of more than 20,000, UNICO supports charitable, scientific and educational projects. It also promotes the Italian heritage and culture and stimulates members to serve their communities. Many of the *Feste Italiane*— celebrations of Italian-American life—are sponsored by local UNICO affiliates for funding their philanthropic efforts. UNICO headquarters are in Bloomfield, New Jersey.

Long after the earlier waves of mass Italian immigration, the American Committee of Italian Migration was formed in 1952 to assist Italian immigrants in dealing with the various legal and social aspects of the immigrant experience and to influence United States immigration policies.

Honoring the significant contributions made by Italian Americans to world sports is the National Italian American Sports Hall of Fame in Arlington Heights, a Chicago suburb.

Italian Americans have always been sensitive to the way they are portrayed in the mass media. To foster a positive image and to promote the production of culturally enriching programs, the Italian American Media Institute in Washington, D.C., was founded by Joseph Giordano.

Italian Americans began their first political activity by banding together to fight prejudice, discrimination, and defamation. As their efforts became successful, they turned their attention to creating a political force. This shift in direction resulted in the founding of the National Italian American Foundation in 1975 by Rev. Geno Baroni, Jeno Paulucci, Frank Stella, and Congressman Frank Annunzio. NIAF, with offices in Washington, D.C., works to unite the nation's twenty million Italian Americans, to support education and cultural activity, and to lobby for Italian-American causes in the national government.

As Italian Americans began entering the professional fields they organized associations around shared fields of specialization.

Two national publications following the literary endeavors of Italian Americans are: *Voices in Italian Americana,* Department of Foreign Languages and Literatures, Purdue University in West Lafayette, Indiana, and *La bella figura,* "the literary journal devoted to Italian-American women," published in San Francisco, California.

A growing national organization of third, fourth, and fifth generation Italian Americans is *Fieri,* founded in 1984 with headquarters in the Bronx, New York City. Chapters in New York, Washington, D.C., Baltimore, Chicago, and San Francisco promote language education and cultural activity. Through networking and exchange programs that foster trips to ancestral homes, *Fieri* represents the present generation's recovery of Italianism.

In everything from economic survival through social and political advancement to cultural preservations, Italian Americans have banded together to enhance their ethnic identity and to contribute to the progress of the entire country.

A few of the organizations are: John D. Calandra Italian American Institute, New York City; the American Italian Renaissance Foundation, New Orleans, Louisiana; the American Association of Teachers of Italian, River Forest, Illinois; the American Italian Historical Association, Staten Island, New York; the American Association of Italian Studies, South Bend, Indiana; the Italian American Labor Council, New York City; the Italian American War Veterans of the United States, Youngstown, Ohio; the National Italian American Bar Association, Washington, D.C.; and the National Organization of Italian-American Women, New York City. Chicago groups band together with an active umbrella organization, the Joint Civic Committee of Italian Americans.

Political and Public Service

Serving humankind through government, education, or science is congenial to the Italian generosity of spirit. Furthermore, the Italian psyche seems to have the resilience to persevere in these sometimes thankless pursuits. Gaetano Lanza's was one such service. He founded the Massachusetts Institute of Technology in 1861 and headed its department of mechanical engineering for 29 years.

Political opportunities began to open for Italian Americans late in the nineteenth century. Francis B. Spinola of New York, who served from 1887 to 1891, and Anthony J. Caminette of California, who served from 1891 to 1895, were the first congressmen of Italian descent.

Andrew Houston Longino was elected Governor of Mississippi in 1900, and in 1905 Charles J. Bonapart became Secretary of the Navy under President Theodore Roosevelt. Bonapart was appointed Attorney General in 1906 and in 1908 he founded the Federal Bureau of Investigation.

The most famous Italian-American politician was Fiorello La Guardia, born in 1882 on New York's east side. He graduated in 1910 from New York University, served in American consulates overseas, was an interpreter at Ellis Island, and was twice wounded while serving in the Army Air Corps in Europe in World War I. La Guardia became a member of Congress in 1916. He was re-elected two years later while on active duty with the Air Corps. Elected to Congress from another district in 1922, he remained there 10 years and became the mayor of New York in 1933. The "Little Flower," as he was called, ran an efficient government and participated vigorously in the lives of his constituents, speaking to them on a weekly radio program. In World War II La Guardia headed the Office of Civilian Defense. After the war he became director general of the United

Nations Relief and Rehabilitation Administration.

Enrico Fermi received a Nobel Prize in 1938 for his experiments with radioactivity. In 1942 he moved from Rome to Chicago to help the all-out effort to produce the atomic bomb, and a year later moved to Los Alamos, New Mexico. Fermi's friend and colleague, Emilio Segre, won the Nobel Prize for physics in 1959.

In 1950, four Italian Americans vied for the mayoralty of New York City, and Vincent Impelliteri won.

The 1950s were good years for Italian-American public servants. In 1951 John Pastore became the senator from Rhode Island. In 1952 John J. Muccio was appointed Ambassador Extraordinary to Korea. In 1956 Alberto D. Rosselini became governor of the state of Washington, John J. Marchi was elected to the New York State Senate, and Foster Furcolo was elected governor of Massachusetts. Michael V. Di Salle became governor of Ohio in 1958.

John A. Volpe became governor of Massachusetts in 1961, winning re-election four years later. In 1967 Peter Rodino, congressman from New Jersey, succeeded in making Columbus Day a national holiday. In 1973 Rodino headed the Nixon impeachment inquiry. Peter Dominici was elected to the Senate from New Mexico in 1972, the year John Volpe became United States Ambassador to Italy. Ella Grasso was elected to congress in 1970 and 1972 and was elected governor of Connecticut in 1974. She was born in 1919 to Italian immigrant parents. Her second term as governor was cut short by her death from cancer in 1980.

In 1968, Francis J. Mugavero was ordained Bishop of the Diocese of Brooklyn, becoming the first Italian-American cleric to lead one of the world's largest dioceses.

Another Italian-American Nobel laureate, Salvador Luria, biology professor at Massachusetts Institute of Technology (MIT), was recognized in 1969 for his discoveries about viruses. Renato Dulbecco of the Salk Institute for Biological Studies, San Diego, California, shared a 1975 Nobel Prize for economics. In 1985 Dr. Franco Modigliani of the MIT faculty won the Nobel Prize for economics.

In 1986 Dr. Rita Levi-Montalcini shared the Nobel Prize in physiology and medicine for her research on nerve cell development. She teaches at Washington University, St. Louis, and holds dual citizenship.

Eleanor Cutri Smeal, born in 1939 at Ashtabula, Ohio, helped found the National Organization of Women. A leader in the feminist movement since 1970, she was the president of NOW from 1977 to 1982 and was elected again to the office in 1985.

The Watergate scandal brought another Italian American to national prominence: Judge John J. Sirica. Born in Waterbury, Connecticut in 1904, Sirica was appointed to the federal bench by President Dwight D. Eisenhower in 1957. He presided over the Watergate trial astutely and fairly.

In 1978 Edmund Pellegrino became president of Catholic University of America, Washington, D.C. Boston-born A. Bartlett Giamatti, president of Yale University, was elected Commissioner of Baseball in 1988.

Mario Cuomo, born in Queens, New York in 1932, served as New York secretary of state from 1974 to 1978, leading a major investigation of nursing home scandals. He was lieutenant governor from 1978 to 1982 before running for governor and winning in 1982. He is remembered for his brilliant opening speech at the 1984 Democratic National Convention. Inspired by the writings of Saint Francis of Assisi and Pierre Teilhard de Chardin, Cuomo believes the creation is still going on, and he's participating in it by working in the political processes of this country.

The 1982 appointment of Joseph Bernadin of Chicago as Cardinal was a boost to Italian-American pride. The son of immigrants from Trentino, he was born in 1928 in Columbia, South Carolina. His skills as a leader brought him consecration to bishop at age 38, then the youngest bishop in the United States. In 1972 he was appointed Archbishop of Cincinnati. His positions on political and social issues have provided a renewed relevancy to United States Catholics and have established him as a strong voice for them.

Another boost to Italian-American pride was the 1984 nomination of Geraldine Ferraro of New York City as the Democratic vice-presidential candidate. She was the first woman and the first Italian American to run for such a high office. Born in 1935, she attended Fordham University School of Law at night while teaching in the public schools during the day. She was elected to the House of Representatives in 1978.

In the 1980s, President Ronald Reagan appointed Antonin Scalia to the supreme court, Frank Carlucci as secretary of defense, and General Carl Vuono as army chief of staff.

Leadership of a different type has come from Lee A. Iacocca, chief executive officer of Chrysler Corporation. Iacocca served as chairman of the Statue of Liberty-Ellis Island Foundation which raised funds for needed restoration of a site where millions of Italian immigrants first touched foot in America, including his own parents in 1921. Born in 1924 in Allentown, Pennsylvania, Lido Anthony Iacocca studied engineering at Lehigh and Princeton. He joined Ford Motor Company as an engineer, became president of the company in 1970, and was fired in 1978 by Henry Ford II. Joining Chrysler, which was losing billions, Iacocca negotiated a government bailout, paid back the loan in record time, and became a best-selling author. By hanging tough in hard times, Lee Iacocca gave America hope.

And speaking of hope, no one offered it better than Charles Atlas (Angelo Siciliano). His body-building course, advertised in comic books, offered to transform 97-pound weaklings into he-men, and it psyched them up so effectively that no one ever kicked sand in their faces again, no matter what they weighed.

Excellence in Sports

The Italian sports tradition reaches from the early Roman athletic contests, which produced a style of wrestling still practiced, to the tough hits at the line of scrimmage by players with Italian names.

Excellence in athletic performance has been recognized in the National Italian American Sports Hall of Fame in Illinois. Founded in 1977 by George R. Randazzo as the Italian American Boxing Hall of Fame, the Hall opened in Elmwood Park and began its all-sports commitment in 1978. Ten years later, the organization purchased a spacious modern facility with seven acres of land in Arlington Heights, Illinois. The Hall of Fame offers scholarships, raising the funds among supporters in thirty-one cities.

Randazzo has the largest, most complete collection of boxing photographs in the nation, started when he was eleven years old. His Uncle Johnny boxed as "the killer" and trained with Rocky Graziano. Randazzo was frequently at ringside to cheer him on.

Boxing was the first sport to attract Italian Americans, producing contenders such as Primo Carnera and Tony Canzoneri. In 1987 the Hall of Fame inducted Harry Jeffra (Ignatius Pasquale Guiffi), bantamweight and featherweight champion in the late 1930s and early 1940s. Jeffra was born in Baltimore in 1914.

Joe DiMaggio, the son of Sicilian immigrants, was the first non-boxer inducted. A rookie with the New York Yankees in 1936, he dazzled the fans with his home runs, runs scored, hits, stolen bases, and batting average. His greatest major league feat was to hit safely in 56 consecutive games in 1941. The "Yankee Clipper" was the first baseball player to command a salary of $100,000 a year. He retired in 1951. DiMaggio also is known as one of the husbands of the glamorous screen star Marilyn Monroe.

The first woman to be inducted into the Hall of Fame was golfer Donna Caponi, in 1981. A well-known celebrity golfer in the Hall of Fame is Ken Venturi. Mary Lou Retton, gymnastics champion of the 1984 Olympics, was named Italian-American Athlete of the Year for that year.

Other inductees to the Hall of Fame include Rocky Marciano (1924-1969), world heavyweight champion in 1952, who grew up in Brockton, Massachusetts, and Vincent Lombardi (1913-1970), the Brooklyn-born coach of the Green Bay Packers known as "the miracle man of football."

Francesco Stefano Pezzolo (1887-1961) was the first Italian-American baseball player in the major leagues. To avoid discrimination, he changed his name to Ping Bodi. He played with the Chicago White Sox from 1911 to 1917 and with the New York Yankees from 1918 to 1921.

Billy Martin, the volatile manager of the New York Yankees, was born Alfred Manuel Pesano in 1928 in Berkeley, California. He began to play in the minor leagues in 1946 and turned to coaching and managing in the 1960s.

Phil Rizzuto, born in Brooklyn in 1918, made it to the majors in 1941 and became "the scooter" of the Yankees. Retiring in 1956, he became a broadcaster for the Yankees.

Tom Lasorda pitched for the Dodgers in the 1950s and became the team's manager in 1976. Born in 1927 in Norristown, Pennsylvania, Lasorda went to Italy in 1974 to instruct baseball coaches. Refusing payment, he said Italy had given him his father, and he wanted to "give something back to Italy."

Joe Garagiola, born in 1926 in St. Louis, Missouri, was a rookie with the St. Louis Cardinals when they won the 1946 world series. He has been a high-profile sports broadcaster since 1955, working in both radio and television.

Yogi Berra, another St. Louis native, was born Lawrence Peter Berra in 1925. He received little encouragement early in his baseball career but became an outstanding hitter and catcher and played in 75 world series games, making 71 world series hits. He managed the Yankees twice. He is remembered for colorful language, including his sage observation that the game "ain't over till it's over," which was quoted by President Ronald Reagan in reference to the 1988 presidential campaign.

Other Italian-American baseball players include Frank Viola, Buddy Biancalana, Tony LaRussa, Paul Noce, Jack Clark, Jim Fregosi, John Cangelosi, Larry Bowa, and Mike Scioscia.

In football, Joseph Michael Bellino, born in 1938 at Winchester, Massachusetts, won the Heisman Trophy in 1960 playing for the United States Naval Academy. Bellino later played three professional football seasons with the Boston Patriots before his retirement.

Franco Harris, born in 1950 in Fort Dix, New Jersey, was the pride and joy of Penn State Coach Joe Paterno and retired in 1984 after 13 years in professional football with the Pittsburgh Steelers. He ranked after Walter Payton and Jim Brown on the all-time rushing list with 12,120 yards, and knew victory in the Super Bowl four times.

Other professional football players include Dan Marino with the Miami Dolphins, Joe Montana with the San Francisco 49ers, Vinny Testaverde with the Tampa Bay Buccaneers, and Mark Bavaro with the New York Giants.

Michael and Mario Andretti uphold ethnic pride in auto racing. Giorgio Chinaglia, born in Carrara, Italy, in 1947, distinguished himself in a ten-year career with the Cosmos professional soccer team, retiring in 1985. In hockey, Tony and Phil Esposito won fame with the Chicago Black Hawks.

One of the most famous jockeys of all time, Eddie Arcaro has ridden five Kentucky Derby winners and won six Preaknesses, six Belmonts and two triple crowns. Born in 1916 in Cincinnati, Ohio, Arcaro started to ride in the late 1920s and retired in 1962, a millionaire many times over, to become a sports commentator.

Other Italian-American sports greats include Linda Frattiane, the Olympic ice-skating champion, and Matt Biondi, who brought home the gold in Olympic swimming.

Hot-air ballooning was a young sport when Ben Abruzzo, in the late 1970s and early 1980s, became the first man to pilot a balloon across the Pacific and Atlantic Oceans. Born in 1930 at Rockford, Illinois, Abruzzo hoped to pilot a balloon around the globe in a single flight, but a plane crash in 1985 ended his dream.

The first Hall of Fame scholarship was given in 1981 by the parents of John J. Jacklin, a lifetime sports enthusiast who at age 23, goalkeeper in a hockey game, suddenly called time, collapsed, and later died at a hospital of a cerebral hemorrhage. His maternal forebears were from Trijano, Brindisi, and Trivigna, Italy. His mother, Estelle Jacklin, now works for the Sports Hall of Fame, and is the Illinois Women's Chapter Vice-president and Scholarship Chairman. Hall of Fame scholarships have helped hundreds of high school seniors to go on to college "to the tune of $500,000," says National Chairman Paul Paoletti.

Red, White & Green Sports, a monthly newspaper established by the National American Sports Hall of Fame Foundation, reaches more than 10,000 members and other sports fans. The Hall of Fame Foundation is a non-profit organization with chapter affiliates in the East, Midwest, South, and West.

Art and Architecture

Italians have never separated use from beauty, architecture from art. From the earliest times, influences have been legion. The Saracen invasion of Sicily in 827 B.C. introduced stiff and formal mosaic art. Norman architecture flowered there later, and eventually a unique blend of Greek, Saracen, Italian, and Roman styles evolved in the Cathedral of Monreale near Palermo.

The legendary founding of Rome by Romulus in 753 B.C. is symbolized by the Etruscan bronze statue of a she-wolf which became an icon of Rome. Images of the suckling male infants, Romulus and Remus, were added in the era of Benvenuto Cellini (1500-1571).

The Etruscans, who came from Asia Minor, admired Greek art, but they added their own ardent, sensual touch to the statuettes, lamps and ornaments that can be seen in archaeological museums today.

By the mid-700s the Greeks were colonizing southern Italy and Sicily. Some of the best-preserved Doric temples in the world can still be seen in Agrigento, Syracuse, Selinunte and Segesta in Sicily, and at Paestum near Naples. Two magnificent bronze statues, the *Warriors of Riace,* were found in 1972 off the coast of Calabria and are now in the Reggio Archaeological Museum.

After the Greeks and the Etruscans came the Republic— the years of struggle leading to the rule of Augustus, the emperor who said he found Rome brick and left it marble. This was the time when the magnificent baths and domed buildings were constructed—with new ease because the secret of concrete had been discovered.

Portraiture had its birth in carved stone during these years. Unlike the Greeks, who idealized their subjects, the

Romans included the warts. The Capitoline Museum in Rome contains these proud heads of the past.

Hadrian erected more buildings than any other Roman emperor. Among his accomplishments were the great Pantheon in Piazza della Rotonda and his own mausoleum, which became the papal fortress of Sant'Angelo. He imported many sculptures and decorations from Greece. Constantine built some of Rome's first churches, and Emperor Theodosius strengthened Christianity as the state religion. The mosaics in the churches of Ravenna created in this period are some of the loveliest in the world.

Romanesque architecture flourished in the city-states during the Middle Ages, as seen in San Zenone at Verona, the cathedrals of Piacenza, Pisa, and Monreale, the Leaning Tower and the baptistery at Pisa, San Stefano at Bologna, San Michele at Lucca, San Pietro and Santa Maria at Tuscania, and the Palatinate Chapel at Palermo.

When the church of Saint Francis of Assisi was consecrated in 1253, the premier painters of the day hurried to Assisi to decorate it, including Cimabue from Florence and Simone Martini from Siena. Giotto's murals can be seen in the Scrovegni Chapel in Padua. Bernard Berenson, the great connoisseur of Italian art, explained that Giotto had "dominion over the significant." The Gothic influence made few inroads in Italy. The Milan cathedral is the only total example of this northern architecture.

The Renaissance, encouraged by the patronage of the Church and men of wealth, such as the Medicis, began in Florence. Its architecture appropriated classical forms, using the human figure on a massive scale for decoration. Ghiberti's *Gate of Paradise* for the cathedral linked the Gothic and the Renaissance, and Donatello created his magnificent *David* in marble. Filippo Brunelleschi (1377-1446) pioneered detailed drawings to replace build-as-you-go planning. He raised a vast dome over Florence Cathedral and created the lovely churches of San Lorenzo and Santo

Spirito plus the original portion of the Pitti Palace. The artistic riches of the Florentine Renaissance were remarkable, including painters like Fra Angelico, noted for delicate color; Andrea del Castagno, known for his dramatic murals; Paolo Uccello of the pure perspective; and Fra Filippo Lippi, distinguished by a quirky individuality.

Elsewhere, Piero della Francesca was painting his mysterious images in Arezzo, Urbino and Borgo, and Antonello da Messina was painting in the Flemish manner in Sicily.

Then came the immortal masters: Sandro Botticelli, who illustrated Dante; Verrocchio, the powerful sculptor; Leonardo da Vinci (1452-1519); Michelangelo Buonarroti (1475-1564); and Raphael Santi (1483-1520).

The first masterpiece of the High Renaissance was Leonardo's mural of *The Last Supper*. Michelangelo was noted for his giant figure of *David,* and Raphael was admired for his idealized images. When Pope Julius II called Michelangelo and Raphael to Rome to decorate the new St. Peter's, Leonardo soon followed. The aging Michelangelo's glorious production of the Sistine ceiling paintings and Raphael's fresco cycle in the Vatican remain.

Mannerism came to the fore in the sixteenth century, and the mysterious and masterful art of Giorgione surfaced in Venice. When Giorgione died of the plague, his pupil, Titian, became the prime mover of the Venetian art scene. His style was sensual. Paolo Veronese (1528-88) brought the classical spirit back and employed radiant color. The Venetian Renaissance ended with the tempestuous color and design of Jacopo Tintoretto's paintings.

The Baroque period is epitomized by the sculpture of Gianlorenzo Bernini (1598-1680), who added the columns to St. Peter's. Canaletto and Guardi, the Venetian view painters, did their pink and blue scenes for tourists to take home, and Tiepolo (1696-1770) dissolved interiors to reveal idealized figures in unfettered space.

Amedeo Modigliani (1884-1920) settled in Paris, where he gave back to line the function it had had for the Italian masters. De Chirico (1888-1978) explored the surreal, and Morandi created still lifes.

Modern architecture claimed Antonio Sant Elia. Avant-gardists called *Nuove Tendenze* all allied with the Futurist movement in poetry and art. Between the world wars, the style was neoclassical. Marcello Piacentini, Mussolini's chief architect, was putting up pompous buildings in Rome. Pier Luigi Nervi was the most promising of the postwar architects, creating exposition halls in Turin, sport palaces in Rome, and a new Papal Audience Hall.

Italian-American artists include Harry Bertoia (1915-1978), whose lyric sculptures almost sing; Constantine Brumidi (1805-1880), who created the allegorical murals in the United States Capitol; and Simon Rodia (1875-1965), folk artist, who created the Watts Towers in Los Angeles of cement, wire, broken bottles, and urban cast-asides.

Frank Stella, born in 1936, is a famous contemporary artist with works in the nation's premier museums. Mark di Suvero, born in 1933, is a sculptor working in materials of weight and substance (railroad ties and steel).

Virginio Ferrari, born in Verona, Italy, came to the United States in 1966 as artist-in-residence and assistant professor of sculpture at the University of Chicago. His huge steel sculpture, *Being Born*, at the corner of State and Washington streets in the Loop, was a gift to the city of Chicago from the Tool & Die Institute in Park Ridge, Illinois.

Ralph Fasanella, born in 1914, was discovered in the early 1970s as "the best American primitive painter since Grandma Moses" and is known for his depiction of working class life and struggles. In his studio in Davenport, Iowa, Ralph Iaccarino paints the exuberant flora of Central America as a metaphor for life. The work of Robert Buono, painter and sculptor, depicts his experiences in the Vietnam War.

When Paolo Soleri, the contemporary Italian-American architect, chose the name "arcology" for his concepts, he was thinking in true Italian terms—of marriage and mingling. Arcosanti, his city of the future, seventy miles north of Phoenix, Arizona, is designed to marry architecture and ecology in an energy-efficient recycling program. The design calls for solar heating and roof cisterns to collect rain water for multiple uses, and a vertically built city that can do without automobiles within its boundaries so the surrounding land can be used as a green belt.

Three Italian artists stormed the New York art scene in the 1980s. Known as "the three C's," Enzo Cucchi, Francesco Clemente, and Sandro Chia were called the *transavanguardia,* translated loosely as postmodernists. Cucchi's works are fierce religious expressions. Clemente creates bizarre erotic images. Chia paints monumental pageantry with intense energy. These three also have been called the "New Romanticists."

Whether it be in the Old World or the New, for Italians and their descendants, the instinct to make art is eternal.

The National Gallery of Art, Washington, D.C., has the best collection of Italian art in the nation. Others with significant holdings are the Metropolitan, New York; the Brooklyn Museum; Baltimore Museum of Art; and Boston Museum of Fine Arts. Corcoran Gallery of Art has a collection of Etruscan antiquities, and Detroit Institute of Arts has Italian art objects.

Literature: a Heritage
by Julie McDonald

Almost two thousand years, strikingly different languages, and totally different viewpoints separate the *Aeneid* of Virgil and *A Coney Island of the Mind* by Lawrence Ferlinghetti, but both works display the passionate vitality of the Italian spirit.

Perhaps Mario Puzo's 1969 novel, *The Godfather,* will not have the staying power of Boccaccio's *Decameron,* a collection of earthy tales told by people fleeing the plague, but it has made its mark on American life. *Speak Softly Love,* the theme song of the film version, is played at many Italian-American weddings.

Early Italian literature was inaccessible to the multitudes because it was written in Latin, but there is a long unbroken line of writers who can be called Italian. Cicero (106-43 B.C.) wrote, "There is nothing so absurd but some philosopher has said it." Horace (65-8 B.C.) observed, "A word once let out of the cage cannot be whistled back again." Virgil's famous *Aeneid* was ten years in the writing and unfinished at his death in 19 B.C. Ovid, the poet of love, was born in 43 B.C., the year Cicero was slain. In *Ars Amatoria* he wrote, "Jupiter from on high laughs at the perjury of lovers."

The grip of Latin was loosened by two forces—the courtly love of ladies and the popular religious revival of the late twelfth and early thirteenth centuries. Some Italian poets adopted Provençal as their language and others, the Sicilian School, wrote in Italian, the everyday speech of the people. The effect of the religious impulse was seen in *Cantico delle Creature* by Saint Francis of Assisi (1182-1226).

The common language flowered in Tuscany in the mid-thirteenth century, and all the linguistic cross-currents came together in the writing of Dante Alighieri (1265-1321).

His *Divine Comedy* remains a matchless masterpiece in which he "gave voice to ten silent centuries," according to Carlyle. The book helped establish the Tuscan dialect as the language of Italy. In the fourteenth century Petrarch became the first great biographer and Boccaccio wrote his bawdy classic, the *Decameron*. In the fifteenth century Florence kept the Italian language alive, particularly in the writings of Lorenzo de Medici, who was called Lorenzo the Magnificent.

Stories and folk tales of the Italians provided William Shakespeare with models and inspiration for several of his plays, such as *Julius Caesar, Romeo and Juliet,* and *The Merchant of Venice.*

During the Renaissance, Ludovico Ariosto wrote the perfect chivalrous romance, *Orlando Furioso.* Prominent women poets included Vittoria Colonna and Gaspara Stampa.

Outside the arena of fiction and poetry was Niccolo Machiavelli (1469-1527), author of *The Prince* and the inspiration for the devil's nickname, "Old Nick." One theme of his book, "the end justifies the means," made it a manual for devious political practices.

Establishment of the Italian Republic in 1871 has been followed by a national literature that includes the works of Ugo Foscolo, Giacomo Leopardi, Allesandro Manzoni, Giosue Carducci, Gabriele D'Annunzio, Grazia Deledda (Nobel Prize winner, 1925), Giovanni Verga, Filippo Tommaso Marinetti, and Luigi Pirandello (Nobel Prize winner, 1934).

Since World War I a sense of disillusionment has pervaded the writing of authors like Alberto Moravia, Vasco Pratolini, Cesare Pavese, Elio Vittorini, and Ignazio Silone, whose *Fontamara* (1930) re-creates the beginning years of Fascist dominance. Other writers of this period include Salvatore Quasimodo (Nobel Prize winner, 1959), Giuseppe Ungaretti, and Eugenio Montale (Nobel Prize winner, 1975).

Carlo Levi was a realist and author of the documentary novel *Christ Stopped at Eboli* (1945). A titled Italian author of recent times, Giuseppe Lampedusa, Duke of Parma, wrote *The Leopard* (1957), a story of Sicilian life in the 1860s. Carlo Emilio Gadda, an experimentalist, wrote *That Awful Mess on Via Merulana*. Umberto Eco's *The Name of the Rose* made the *New York Times* best-seller list in 1983.

Though the Italian influence on American letters can be found throughout early American literature, the first Italian-American writers who achieved any measure of popular or critical success in America came from families whose background was in the southern Italian oral traditions rather than in Italian literary traditions. Individual writers have surfaced now and then since the 1930s, yet few have been able to capture national attention as did Mario Puzo with *The Godfather* in 1969. Born in New York's Hell's Kitchen, Puzo disproved his family's belief that "only a son of the nobility could possibly be a writer." Though he is more proud of his novels *The Dark Arena* (1955) and *The Fortunate Pilgrim* (1965), Mario Puzo will be remembered for his portrayal of the Corleone mafiosi.

Writers of Italian descent whose works have stood the test of time include Arturo Giovannitti, John Fante, Pietro DiDonato, Jerre Mangione, and Joseph Tusiani. Giovannitti, poet and union organizer, came to the United States at the age of sixteen and was a coal miner and ditch-digger. His poetry recalls the trials and triumphs of early Italian immigrants. The famous H. L. Mencken, editor of *The American Mercury*, fostered the career of Fante, whose novels, *Wait Until Spring, Bandini!* (1938), *Ask the Dust* (1939), and *Brotherhood of the Grape* (1977) form a definitive saga of the Italian-American experience.

In 1939 DiDonato, a young Italian-American writer, son of immigrants in Rochester, New York, took the American literary scene by storm with his novel *Christ in Concrete,* the story of a family surviving the death of its patriarch. Tusiani, a poet, translator and scholar who studied English in

Italy, used his new language in much of his poetry and so gave voice to the immigrants who came before him. His *Gente Mia* (1978) is a classic.

Mount Allegro, a book that has remained in print since its publication in 1942, tells of life in a Rochester, New York "Little Italy" and established Jerre Mangione as a prominent voice in American literature. Mangione, who served on the national WPA writers project (*The Dream and the Deal,* unpublished until 1972), brought a more sophisticated flair to Italian-American story-telling and also wrote books on his experiences traveling to his parents' homeland in Sicily (*Reunion in Sicily,* 1950), and *The World Around Danilo Dolci,* 1968.

The end of World War II brought a new wave of Italian immigration. In 1960, one writer left Italy with the intention of establishing himself in America, where his grandfather had found work. Giose Rimanelli revolutionized the idea of what it means to be an Italian-American writer and forged a new bridge between Italy and America. His Italian novels became best-sellers in translation. *Original Sin* (1957) dealt with an Italian's unfulfilled dream of escaping to a better life in America.

John Ciardi, poet, essayist, Harvard professor, poetry editor of *The Saturday Review* and translator of Dante, was born in Boston to parents from Avellino. He contributed forty books of poetry and criticism before his death in 1986.

Lawrence Ferlinghetti, born Lawrence Ferling in Yonkers, New York, restored his Italian surname and achieved prominence as a poet, publisher, and proprietor of the first paperback bookstore in the United States. City Lights Books in San Francisco became a Mecca for followers of the Beat Movement of the 1950s. Ferlinghetti was arrested on obscenity charges for publishing what would become an American classic, Allen Ginsberg's *Howl.* Two other major figures in the Beat Movement—poets Gregory Corso and Diane DiPrima—are Italian Americans. Corso, born in New

York's Little Italy, spent time in orphanages and prisons before publishing his many volumes of poetry.

Gay Talese, whose parents came from southern Italy, writes non-fiction, including *Honor Thy Father* (1971).

With the publication of *Blood of My Blood* in 1974, Richard Gambino presented the first popular study of what it meant to be Italian American. This book, a best seller, was responsible for setting off the third generation's search for ancestral roots. Gambino also published *Vendetta*, a historical account of the 1891 lynching of eleven Italians in New Orleans that nearly triggered a war with Italy, and *Bread and Roses* (1981), a fictional portrayal of the highlights of Italian-American history.

That last title has a history all its own. "We Want Bread—and Roses, Too" was a sign carried in 1912 by young, economically exploited Italian-American women striking a textile mill in Lawrence, Massachusetts. The phrase "Bread and Roses" became the title of a poem written about the strike and set to music. Arturo Giovanitti wrote an Italian song, *Pan e Rose,* which was popular with members of the Italian Dressmakers Local 89 of the International Ladies Garment Union. The 1912 strike resulted in national sympathy for the exploited Italian workers in America.

The successful and rapid assimilation of Italians into the American mainstream liberated many Italian-American women from their traditional roles. *Umbertina* (1979), Helen Barolini's first novel, dramatized the plights of three generations of Italian-American women. Barolini is responsible for casting light on the previously shadowed work of Italian-American women writers with the publication of her 1986 American Book Award winning anthology *The Dream Book,* which was the first book-length anthology of Italian-American writers.

Italian-American women writers who have had an impact on American poetry include Diane DiPrima, Maria Gillan, Sandra Gilbert, and Daniela Gioseffi.

Italian Americans boast two recent winners of the prestigious Flannery O'Connor award for collections of short stories: Tony Ardizzone for *The Evening News* (1985) and Salvatore LaPuma for *Boys of Bensonhurst* (1986).

Tina DeRosa's *Paper Fish* (1980), Jay Parini's *The Patch Boys* (1986), Kenny Marotta's *A Piece of Earth* (1985), Josephine Gattuso Hendin's *The Right Thing to Do* (1987) and Anthony Giardina's *A Boy's Pretensions* (1987) are examples of the coming of age of Italian-American writers.

Today, more than ever before, Italian-American authors are beginning to meet and know each other and to support each other's work. Even Italian-American organizations, once established for mutual aid and economic survival of *paesani* and their families, are shifting their focus from life insurance to a broader base that can include artistic support. The Order Sons of Italy and the National Italian American Foundation are just two of the many organizations offering college scholarships that enable young writers to pursue literary studies and careers.

The first representative anthology of creative and critical writings by and about Italian Americans is *From Margin to Mainstream: Writings in Italian Americana* (Purdue University Press), edited by Anthony J. Tamburri, Paolo Giordano and Fred L. Gardaphe. The book includes a comprehensive bibliography of publications by Italian Americans. Amerital UNICO has paved the way for recognition of the achievements of Italian-American writers by sponsoring national literary contests which enable young Italian-American writers to find both acceptance and support.

Collectively the work of Italian-American writers could be viewed as a bible of Italian-American culture. Individually, as American writers, they have added new dimensions to the exploration of what it means to be American.

Film and Theater Greats

Because it belongs to the whole world, we tend to forget the Italian origin of Walt Disney's 1939 animation of *Pinocchio,* a wonderful tale written by Carlo Collodi in 1881. The Florentine journalist, whose real name was Carlo Lorenzini, created Pinocchio, a puppet carved by old Geppetto from a magic piece of firewood. After many harrowing adventures, Pinocchio learns to read and write and is rewarded by being turned into a real boy. The book was first published in translation in the United States in 1892.

Since Pinocchio's American debut Italian-Americans have become a driving force in American cinema. Francis Ford Coppola's epics *The Godfather I* and *II* (1972, 1974) are among the most successful films in American history. Coppola was born in 1939 in Detroit, the son of a composer and musician, and grew up in a New York City suburb. He studied film at U.C.L.A. Among his successful productions are *American Graffiti* (1973), *Apocalypse Now* (1978), and *The Black Stallion* (1979).

Often mentioned in the same breath with Coppola is Martin Scorsese, who made the controversial film, *The Last Temptation of Christ.* He was born in 1942 in Queens, New York City, and grew up in Little Italy. Educated at New York University, he taught several years before starting to pursue realism on film. *Mean Streets* (1973), *Alice Doesn't Live Here Anymore* (1975), *Taxi Driver* (1976) and *Raging Bull* (1979) established his reputation, and he continues to explore the obsessions that drive us to victories or defeats.

Michael Cimino is the third new-wave film director of Italian descent to earn wide public attention. *The Deer Hunter,* his 1978 Vietnam picture, won five Oscars. Born in 1943, he grew up in New York City and on Long Island and was graduated from Yale University. He also directed *Heaven's Gate,* released in 1980 and less favorably received.

The vision of these three men differs widely from that of an earlier Italian-American director, Frank Capra. Born in 1897 in Palermo, Sicily, Capra came to San Francisco with his family when he was six. He graduated in chemical engineering from the California Institute of Technology and joined the Army. His triumphs were happy pictures such as *It Happened One Night* (1934), *Mr. Deeds Goes to Town* (1936), *You Can't Take It With You* (1938), and *It's a Wonderful Life* (1947).

Vincente Minnelli directed Oscar-winning musicals—*An American in Paris,* best picture, 1951; *The Bandwagon,* best picture and best director, 1953; *Gigi,* best picture and best director, 1958. Minnelli married actress Judy Garland in 1945. On stage since age 3, their daughter Liza Minnelli followed in her parents' footsteps and in 1972 won an Academy Award for best actress in *Cabaret.*

Brian De Palma, born in Philadelphia in 1941, specializes in horror films. His first commercial success was *Carrie* (1976), based on a Stephen King novel, and more recently he made *The Untouchables.*

In Italy, postwar film-makers achieved a special gritty realism with a documentary approach as well as a sophisticated view of the mores of the day. Roberto Rossellini's *Open City* (1945) received high praise. He is as well remembered for his conquest of Ingrid Bergman, the Swedish film star, during the making of *Stromboli.* Their daughter, Isabella Rossellini, has won rave reviews as an actress.

Vittorio de Sica's first postwar triumph was *The Bicycle Thief* (1948). His 1956 picture *The Roof* showed his compassion and eye for telling detail in the story of impoverished newlyweds in Rome.

In the 1960s a more puritanical attitude toward films evolved in Italy. Luchino Visconti's *Rocco and His Brother,* which had won top prizes in international film competitions, was criticized for its explicit sex, and Federico Fellini's 1960 film, *La Dolce Vita,* received the same treatment.

Michelangelo Antonioni produced *La Notte* and *Eclipse* in 1962. In the same year Federico Fellini, Luchino Visconti, and Vittorio de Sica worked together to produce *Boccaccio 70.* Another memorable picture of that year was Pietro Germi's *Divorce—Italian Style.*

Bernardo Bertolucci, regarded as the most lyrical Marxist film-maker, made *Before the Revolution* in 1964, and the Oscar-winning *The Last Emperor,* filmed in China in 1986-1987. The late Sergio Leone invented the "spaghetti westerns," cowboy pictures directed and filmed in Italy.

Any list of Italian-American stars must begin with Rudolph Valentino, born in Castellaneta, Italy, in 1895. He came to New York in 1913 and arrived in Hollywood in 1917. When he played the lead in *The Four Horsemen of the Apocalypse,* the Latin lover image was fixed. Women loved him in *The Sheik* and in the eight pictures that followed before his 1926 death at thirty-one from a perforated ulcer.

Jimmy Durante was born to Italian immigrant parents in 1893 on the lower east side of New York. His mother came from Salerno. He dropped out of school in the seventh grade to play honky-tonk piano, formed a band, and opened Club Durante. Vaudeville was the next step, and he went from the Broadway stage to Hollywood. By 1950 he had his own radio show. A raspy voice and the huge "schnozzola," insured by Lloyd's of London, enhanced his comedy routines.

Another notable Italian-American comic was Lou Costello (1906-1959), the pudgy half of the comedy team Abbott and Costello.

Don Ameche, a Hollywood fixture for decades, will be forever remembered for his portrayal of Alexander Graham Bell, inventor of the telephone, in *The Story of Alexander Graham Bell* (1939). Ameche won an Oscar in 1985 for his role in *Cocoon.*

Sophia Loren, born out of wedlock in a Naples slum, appeared in some forgettable Italian movies before trying her luck in Hollywood in 1957. She won an Academy Award for her performance in Vittorio De Sica's *Two Women* in 1961, and she continues to be one of the world's most striking women. Marcello Mastroianni, who has played everything from suave lover to labor organizer, has also achieved lasting fame. Anna Magnani's darkly brooding features have long been familiar to American film fans. She starred in *The Rose Tattoo,* for which she won an Academy Award in 1955, and in *Wild Is the Wind* with Anthony Quinn in 1958.

New York-born Ben Gazzara, a stage and film actor capable of conveying serious menace, won the Drama Critics' Award for his performance in *End as a Man,* and appeared in the film *Al Capone* (1974).

Two intense Italian-American actors born in the 1940s began to dominate films from the late 1960s on: Al Pacino, born in the south Bronx, who starred in *The Godfather* and *Scarface* (1983), and Robert De Niro from the lower east side, who played the psychopathic cabbie in *Taxi Driver* and appeared in *The Godfather, Part II*, *The Deer Hunter, Raging Bull,* and many other films.

Actors of a different type are Sylvester Stallone, born in New York City's Hell's Kitchen in 1946 and famous for *Rocky* (1976) and *Rambo* (1985, based on the book *First Blood*) and their sequels; Alan Alda of *M*A*S*H* fame, born in New York in 1936; and John Travolta, born in Englewood, New Jersey in 1954 and rocketed to fame by *Saturday Night Fever* (1977) and the television series *Welcome Back, Kotter.*

Anne Bancroft's portrayal of the Irish Annie Sullivan in *The Miracle Worker* (1959) and the Anglo-sounding name she traded for her own, Anna Maria Italiano, hide her ethnic origins from many. She was born in the east Bronx in 1931 and has collected several Tony awards and an Oscar. She's remembered as Mrs. Robinson in *The Graduate* with Dustin Hoffman.

Bernadette Peters was born Bernadette Lazzaro in Queens in 1949. A dancer, singer, and actress, she has appeared on Broadway and in movies. In 1984 she played the female lead in the Broadway musical *Sunday in the Park with George.*

Other actresses recognized for their beauty are Virna Lisi, sometimes called "the Italian Marilyn Monroe"; Gina Lollobrigida; Claudia Cardinale; Morgan Brittany; Valerie Bertinelli; Susan Lucci (seen on the soap operas); and Mary Elizabeth Mastroantonio.

The movies of both Italy and America have their roots in the history of Italian theater. Like the literature of Italy, modern theater began in the thirteenth century when parts of the church service were dramatized. Devils and souls of the damned provided the comedy. The form was so popular that the first secular play, Angelo Poliziano's *Orfeo* (fifteenth century), was modeled on it.

Renaissance interest in Greek and Roman comedy and tragedy led to Latin and Italian dramas based on the classic works of Plautus and Seneca. For instance, Niccolo Machiavelli (1469-1527) wrote a suggestive comedy of manners, *La Mandragola,* and Giovanni Cinzio (1504-1573) imitated Seneca in *Orbecche.* Pastoral plays, in vogue all over Europe, also were popular.

The *commedia dell'arte* (masked comedy) developed during the seventeenth century, when artistic production in all fields had nearly ceased. This was the theater of the people, using stock characters and improvisation. The masked characters were Pulcinella, a Neopolitan; the pedantic Doctor, a Venetian; Arlecchino and Colombina, Stenterello and Pasquino, each speaking the dialect of his native city in the slapstick proceedings. Eventually people tired of the standard jokes and plots, and the *commedia dell'arte* waned.

A Venetian comic playwright stood ready to rescue elements of the form. Carlo Goldoni (1707-1793) wrote a number of plays, including *The Mistress of the Inn,* inspired by the masked improvisations.

The eighteenth-century flowering of Italian drama also involved the works of Pietro Metastasio (1698-1782) in melodrama and the tragic plays of Vittorio Alfieri (1749-1803). Gluck, Mozart, and Handel set Metastasio's pieces to music, and Alfieri's lofty work founded a new school.

The *Risorgimento*—the movement for the liberation and unification of Italy, taking place in the late eighteenth century and most of the nineteenth— saw dramas inspired by Italy's history. Alessandro Manzoni (1785-1873) wrote *Adelchi. The Falconer of Pietro Ardena* was written by Niccolini, da Brescia, and Marenco.

Gabriele D'Annunzio (1863-1938) carried the romantic tradition into the twentieth century with plays like *La Gioconda,* popular throughout the world. D'Annunzio was contemporary with the great Italian actress, Eleonora Duse (1858-1924), judged by George Bernard Shaw to be superior to Sarah Bernhardt.

The last quarter of the nineteenth century was devoted to naturalistic dramas and the theater of ideas. Giuseppe Giacosa (1847-1943), Enrico Annibale Butti (1868-1912), and Roberto Bracco (1862-1943) wrote problem plays. A revival of dialect plays in Venice, Milan, Naples, Florence, and Rome created a new vitality in the theaters.

The years between the great wars were dominated by Luigi Pirandello (1867-1936), a Sicilian playwright and Nobel laureate who has been called "the father of modern theater." His best known plays are *Six Characters in Search of an Author, Enrico IV, Tonight We Improvise,* and *Right You Are, If You Think You Are.* His plays dramatized the search for philosophical reality.

In 1909 Fillipo Marinetti published his futurist manifesto celebrating mechanization, irrationality and militarism. Italian fascism had its roots in this movement, and when fascism and Mussolini came to power in the 1920s, dramatic art was suppressed.

As in film, the end of World War II brought a wave of realism to the Italian stage. Eduardo De Filippo's plays delved into the realities of postwar poverty, prostitution, and desperation. Dario Fo and his wife, Franca Rame, have written plays performed all over the western world.

The immigrant theater in the United States featured plays like *Cavalleria Rusticana* (later to become an opera) performed in New York and Chicago.

Italian themes have been adopted by American playwrights in dramas such as Arthur Miller's *A View From the Bridge* and Sidney Howard's *They Knew What They Wanted,* which became the 1956 musical *The Most Happy Fella.*

Contemporary Italian-American playwrights include Frank Melcori, Lionel Bottari, Nicolas Patricca, and Albert Innaurato.

Manteo Marionettes

The life-sized figures of the Manteo Sicilian Marionette Theatre, which provided engrossing entertainment in New York's Little Italy in the 1920s, have become a unique and treasured American folk art.

Agrippino Manteo came to America from Sicily with a few marionettes. Working as an electrician by day, he staged performances by night. His wife, Caterina, collected quarters at the door and their children worked backstage and cranked the pianola.

In the 1950s Mike Manteo, an electrician like his father before him, found that long years in storage had left the marionettes in disrepair. He refurbished them, and today mounts performances at schools and festivals and at his studio/workshop/theater under the Staten Island Museum of Arts and Science. Five generations of Manteos have been involved in the marionette theater that opened in Little Italy in 1923, performing the medieval saga *Orlando Furioso* in 394 nightly episodes stretching over thirteen months.

Dancing Italian

The first ballet was created by an Italian, Baltazarini de Belgioioso, who produced *Ballet Comique de la Reine* for Catherine de' Medici in 1581, and an Italian American, Gerald Arpino, is on the cutting edge of contemporary dance as artistic director of the Joffrey Ballet.

Marie Taglioni, famous for perfecting dancing *en pointe,* appeared in the first Romantic ballet, *Les Sylphides,* choreographed by her father, Filippo, and performed at the Paris Opera in 1832. Taglioni often visited her relatives in Naples, but she refused to dance there because of a papal requirement that female dancers wear blue drawers.

After a successful dance career, Carlo Blasis settled in Milan as director of the Royal Academy of the Dance at La Scala. In 1830 he published *The Code of Terpsichore,* the first systemization of ballet technique.

Enrico Cecchetti (1850-1928) was an Italian dancer who became the ballet teacher of Nijinsky and Pavlova.

The black swan *Pas de Deux* in the third act of *Swan Lake* was devised to showcase the talents of Pierina Legnani, the first ballerina to execute its famous 32 *fouettes.*

The Joffrey Ballet

The Joffrey Ballet was founded in 1956 by Robert Joffrey, the son of an Italian mother and a father from Afghanistan. Joffrey's death at the age of 57 in 1988 put the company's future in the hands of Gerald Arpino, who was born into a large Italian-American family on Staten Island in 1928.

Gerald Arpino's brothers and sisters won ballroom dancing trophies, and he became a chorus boy at the Latin Quarter. In the 1940s he met Leonide Massine, the premier choreographer of the period. Arpino attended Wagner College on Staten Island, then joined the Coast Guard at the end of World War II.

Arpino first encountered Robert Joffrey in a ballet class with Ivan Novikoff. The Russian told Arpino, "You must dance!" From that point on, the two young men pursued the dance in the studios of Mary Ann Wells and Balanchine's School of American Ballet. Balanchine gave Joffrey $500 to form his own company and also gave him some of his ballets.

Arpino did some choreography, but this was not his principal interest until he broke his back dancing in a Seattle Opera production of *Aida* in 1963. As artistic director of the Joffrey succeeding its founder, he intends to continue his choreography, which is a unique mix of modern dance and ballet.

Folk Dancing

Rose Grieco of Montclair, New Jersey, is an American authority on Italian folkways. Her parents came from Potenza, Italy, and she studied music, dramatics, and dance at La Sevilla School of Dancing and the Feagan School of Dramatic Arts in New York City.

Fearing the loss of Italian music and dancing in American life, Grieco organized the Italian Folklore Group of Montclair in 1948. She made seven trips to Italy, Sicily, and Sardinia to research music, dances, and costumes of various provinces and to collect rare percussion instruments such as the *sciatevaisse* (a grooved wooden pole played with a stick) from Capri, and the rare *cian-ciane* (a donkey's collar with a hundred tiny bells and mirrors played during dancing) from Sicily.

Grieco is a charter member of the Italian Folk Arts Federation of America and has taught dances to leaders of Italian groups throughout the United States and Canada. Her most recent performance with the Italian Folklore Group was during the 1988 Columbus Day festivities at the Arena in New Jersey. President Ronald Reagan was in the audience.

Research by Grieco on the Italian dance known as the *tarantella* traces it back to the time of Plato, who described a "frenzy of dancing" engaged in as therapy. The name of the dance derives from Taranto (formerly Tarantula), a seaport in southern Italy where the dance originated. It was believed that the bite of the tarantula spider caused the victim to dance wildly, promoting the expulsion of the venom through the skin.

St. Vitus, an early Christian martyr who came from the region where tarantulas were frequently found, prayed for power to cure anyone afflicted with the dancing mania, and a voice from heaven told him, "Vitus, thy prayer is granted." Pilgrims of the Middle Ages came to his churches to be cured.

A pure *tarantella* is completely improvised to the beat of a tambourine with spontaneous singing. The spirit of the *tarantella* inspired music by Chopin, Mendelssohn, Liszt, and Rossini.

Today, choreographed *tarantellas* are exciting dances whose therapeutic origins are largely forgotten. Dallas, Texas, has a group called the Tarantella Dancers, members of the Italian Folk Art Federation of America. The Federation was organized in Philadelphia in 1977 "to encourage interest and participation in the joyful folk arts of Italy and to make these a part of the ever-evolving culture of America." It claims about thirty-five performing entities in Maryland, Pennsylvania, Minnesota, Virginia, Ohio, Louisiana, New York, Massachusetts, Wisconsin, New Jersey, Illinois, Michigan, Texas, California, Iowa, and West Virginia, plus Ontario and Quebec in Canada.

I Campagnoli of Pittsburgh, directed by Jane Ferro, is a high-profile Italian folk song and dance troupe that made its debut in 1965 and has performed in Italy at Venice, Florence, Lucca, and Rome. The Mayor and Ambassador of Rome presented the group with the Medal of Peace. The players have performed in many American cities and at Epcot Center in Florida. Their prayer is "God bless our beloved Italia; may her skies always be sunny." *I Campagnoli* means "the country folk of Italy."

Teaching the World to Sing

From the Gregorian chant to Luciano Pavarotti, one of the premier operatic tenors of the present day, Italy has given the world a rich gift of *bel canto* (beautiful singing). In a country where stevedores and cab drivers sing arias, music appreciation is a fact of life.

Pope Gregory (590-604) was responsible for the plainchant of the Roman Catholic Church, and the liturgical dramas of the Middle Ages were the ancestors of opera.

In the fourteenth century, Italians were creating flowing melodies for songs about hunting and fishing and the marketplace. Francesco Landini, the blind organist-composer, created three-part songs called *ballatas* that appealed to a secular public. Instruments of the period were vielles, lutes, psaltries, portative organs, flutes, shawms, trumpets, horns, small bells, and cymbals. Clavichords and harpsichords would find wide use in the fifteenth century.

The famous violin makers of Cremona included the Amati family working in the sixteenth and seventeenth centuries. Nicolo Amati, the teacher of Antonio Stradivari, is considered the greatest of them, and Andrea Amati is credited with the design of the present-day instrument. Stradivari (1644-1737) is the most celebrated of Italian violin makers. Of more than 1,000 violins, violas, and cellos that he made, more than 600 survive. The first of the violin-making Guarneris, Andrea (1626-98), was Stradivari's fellow student in the Amati workshop. The most illustrious Guarneri, Giuseppe del Gesù (1687-1745), produced instruments with greater warmth and sonority but less brilliance than the "Strads."

Claudio Monteverdi (1567-1643) created the bridge from the Renaissance to the Baroque period with his madrigals which expressed the state of the soul—the "affections."

Monteverdi's *La Favola d'Orfeo,* performed in Mantua in 1607, was the world's first significant opera performance.

The first opera house in the world, Teatro San Cassiano, opened in Venice in 1637. By the end of the seventeenth century opera was the leading musical endeavor in Italy.

At the same time, Alessandro Scarlatti (1660-1725) was composing art songs and cantatas. Domenico Scarlatti, the son of Alessandro, lived for years in the royal court of Spain, and his compositions show that influence.

Arcangelo Corelli (1653-1713) made a strong mark on chamber music. Antonio Vivaldi (circa 1678-1741) composed opera music and baroque concertos and sonatas.

A Florentine instrument maker, Bartolomeo Cristofori (1655-1730), created a revolutionary new instrument, the piano, around 1709. His piano mechanism was so efficient that it remained unchanged for nearly a century.

Italy influenced Wolfgang Amadeus Mozart, who brought Italian opera to its peak in the eighteenth century with *The Marriage of Figaro, Don Giovanni,* and *Cosi fan Tutti.*

The fame of Gioacchino Rossini (1792-1868) became established in 1813 with his comic operas, including *The Barber of Seville.* Vincenzo Bellini (1801-1835) and Gaetano Donizetti *(1797-1848)* were also prolific opera composers. Giuseppe Verdi (1813-1901), focused on opera as human drama. His best-loved operas are *Rigoletto, Il Trovatore* and *La Traviata.*

One of Italy's most remarkable violinists was Niccolò Paganini (1782-1840). Self-taught, Paganini had an almost demonic flair that influenced Franz Liszt.

Opera of the late nineteenth century followed the *verismo* style, dramatizing familiar situations. Pietro Mascagni's *Cavalleria Rusticana* in 1890 and Ruggiero Leoncavallo's *I Pagliacci* in 1892 exemplified the type. At the turn of the century, Giaccomo Puccini (1858-1924), who wrote *Madame Butterfly,* was all the rage. In the present century, Italian music has followed the trend into 12-tone and expressionistic composition, but the public prefers the old classics.

The Italian language is still used for tempo indications *(allegro)* and dynamics *(forte, piano)* on musical scores as well as for forms like the *sonata, toccata, fugue* and *sinfonia.*

Italian folk music embraces everything from the Anglo-Scottish-sounding songs of the Piedmont to the lyric story-telling ballads of southern Italy.

Among the famous Italian musicians well-known to Americans are Enrico Caruso (1873-1921), the Neapolitan tenor; opera divas Adelina Patti and Amelita Galli-Curci; Arturo Toscanini (1867-1957), the legendary conductor of the NBC Symphony Orchestra who was born in Parma; Mario Lanza, considered by some to have inherited the mantle of Caruso; Anna Maria Alberghetti, who made her Carnegie Hall debut in 1950; and Ezio Pinza, the Metropolitan Opera bass-baritone, who played opposite Mary Martin in *South Pacific.* Riccardo Muti conducts the La Scala Orchestra and the Philadelphia Orchestra.

Gian-Carlo Menotti, born in 1911 and trained in Italy and the United States, has contributed a beloved Christmas custom to his adopted country, the yearly performance of his 1951 opera *Amahl and the Night Visitors* by amateur and professional groups. Norman Dello Joio, born in New York City in 1913, won a Pulitzer Prize in 1957 for his composition, "Meditations on Ecclesiastes."

Italian Americans have dominated the field of American popular music for decades.

Dino Crocetti from Steubenville, Ohio, became Dean Martin, the laid-back crooner who commanded serious money as a Las Vegas entertainer and as a recording artist.

Tony Bennett, born Antonio Dominick Benedetto in Astoria, Queens, New York, in 1926, planned to be a commercial artist, but a stint of singing with a military band changed his direction. He was popular in the early 1950s, was shoved aside by rock-and-roll, and made a 1962 comeback with the song that became his signature, "I Left My Heart in San

Francisco." He still paints and sells his art at hefty prices.

Chuck Mangione, born in 1940 in Rochester, New York, enjoyed eating spaghetti with Dizzy Gillespie when he was a kid and grew up to produce his own brand of jazz. His composition "Feels So Good" was a big hit of the late 1970s and early 1980s, and his record albums are top sellers.

Cool jazz was the specialty of Lennie Tristano, who was born in Chicago in 1919 and died in 1978. He became blind at the age of nine, but studied piano and later added clarinet and saxophone to begin a professional career in his teens. He was one of the first free-form improvisation musicians.

Frank Sinatra, born in 1915 in Hoboken, New Jersey, has a Sicilian background. He caused the young female population to swoon in the 1940s and went on to prove that he was a fine dramatic actor in *From Here to Eternity* (1953) and *The Man with the Golden Arm* (1956). Sinatra retired in 1971 but, like the great actress Sarah Bernhardt, he couldn't make it stick.

Rounding out the list of Italian-American entertainers who have had what it takes to charm the masses are Julius La Rosa, the durable Perry Como, Vic Damone, Caterina Valente, Mario Lanza, Connie Francis, Frankie Valli, Bobby Darrin, Felix Papilardi, Bruce Springsteen, Sonny Bono, and Madonna.

In Guy Lombardo's era, the 1930s and 1940s, New Year's Eve was never complete without the smooth strains of his music. Equally smooth was the music of Henry Mancini. Frankie Laine earned fame with his rousing "Mule Train," and Frank Zappa blasted away with his rock group, Mothers of Invention.

The Italian American known to all professional musicians was James C. Petrillo, who retired in 1958 as president of the American Federation of Musicians.

Traditional Italian folk music and theater flourish in New York City, thanks to *i Giullari di Piazza,* co-founded by Alessandra Belloni, its artistic director, and John La Bar-

bera, music director and composer. The company's reper-
toire is rich in the folkloric traditions of southern Italy from
the Middle Ages to the present. Actors and actresses, sing-
ers, dancers, and musicians perform *La Lupa* (The She-
wolf), *Don Giovanni, Danza dei Setteveli* (Dance of the Seven
Veils, anonymous from the twelfth century), *The Legend of
the Madonna of Casandrino,* traditional love songs from
Sicily, and many others.

*i Giullari Di Piazza, New York City Italian folk music and
theater company features, in foreground, Alessandra Belloni, artistic director and founder, and on the far right, John
La Barbera, music director, composer, and co-founder.*

Religion and the Festa

by Don Fiore

Festa di San Gennaro

From Santa Rosalia in Monterey, California to San Gennaro on New York City's Mulberry Street, religious festivals bring street processions, Italian symphonic bands, carnivals, and an aura of celebration.

Each event is an Italian import from the years of mass emigration by Neapolitans, Sicilians, Calabresi and others from Italy's rural south. In an amazing show of endurance, these religious festivals have survived the rigors of transplantation to alien locales, and the hostility of both Protestants and non-Italian Catholics. Remarkably, they have withstood the test of time, altered by little more than the necessary physical adjustments to modern American settings. These Italian street festivals represent some of the most ancient traditions observable in this country today.

The feast of Our Lady of Mount Carmel in Melrose Park, a Chicago suburb, which I attended with a few friends, is one of the nation's oldest. Local tradition claims that since its inception in 1894 the celebration's Sunday street procession, known erroneously to some as "the Italian parade," has never been canceled because of rain.

The procession was impressive. One by one, the various religious societies solemnly passed in file, each with its banner held high like the standard leading the Roman legionnaires. Other groups carried *cente tabernacoli,* portable shrines that, with their elaborate tiers of ribbons, flowers, and candles, presented a delicate wedding-cake appearance.

The life-size statue of the Blessed Virgin and her Divine Infant, borne on the shoulders of half a dozen long-robed male devotees, was still a few blocks away. My friends and I could gauge its distance by the echoes of firecrackers and the faint crash of cymbals issuing from the thirty-five-piece band that accompanied it.

Suddenly, there arose the cry, "She's coming! Our lady! La Madonna!"

On every block the statue's approach was heralded by the same contagious sense of anticipation that quickened the hearts of even those who had witnessed this unchanging ritual year after year over the course of a lifetime.

To the north, the cheerful chaos of carnival reigned over Twenty-third Street. Normally a quiet stretch of large frame homes, broken only briefly by the presence of Our Lady of Mt. Carmel Church, it had even changed its name for the occasion. For five days, it had been "Via del Carmine."

Arches of colored lights and shimmering garlands spanned the street for blocks, sparkling in the sunlight and promising even more magnificence upon the arrival of night. Beneath them, vendors offered food and souvenirs from canvas tents, push carts, and ramshackle wooden booths crammed into every niche and corner. A smoky haze hovered over the street, carrying the aromas of charcoal-roasted sausage, fried peppers and tomato sauce rich with oregano and basil. Not a hot dog or hamburger in sight! Nothing but an endless array of beef sandwiches, pizza, stuffed artichokes, deep-fried *calamari,* fresh clams on the half-shell, Italian ices, *cannoli,* and Italian beans, *ceci* and *lupini.*

Carnival rides towered over the adjoining streets. The amusement stands, sandwiched everywhere in between, were crowded with teen-age marksmen setting their aims on targets to win stuffed animals for their girlfriends. A large, fading photograph of the Saint's image, captioned with the words *Madonna del Carmine* spelled out in lights, hung above the church entrance. Over the past week tens of thousands had made their pilgrimage through these doors, lighting candles at the nightly novenas, then returning to the street to mill about shoulder to shoulder and savor the food or play the games. The border between playing and praying was never clearly defined. Even under the arches, the resplendent symbols of revelry, nearby homeowners had set up shrines in their front yards. Plaster statues of a regiment of saints stood along with photographs of deceased family members beneath small, red silk canopies or around fountains outlined by strings of glimmering lights.

Back on Twenty-first Street, an ear-shattering fusillade of M-80s thundered around us. Smaller than bombs, but larger than firecrackers, they filled the air with a dense residue of smoke and the smell of gunpowder. Snare drums snapped brisk afterbeats as the band, becoming ever more audible over the reverberations of the bombs, reached the glorious finale of a symphonic march. The image of God's Mother was approaching, her cape and golden tresses moving gently in the slight breeze. Fair skinned and lovely in regal array, she gazed forward with stunningly life-like eyes as if surveying in benevolent silence the massive display of veneration offered to her.

At her feet were stacked sacks of money that had been collected along the procession's winding way, grateful repayments for favors received or for prayers answered. Toddlers, hoisted up by parents, stretched their tiny arms to touch her gown. Following tightly behind the statue, like children clinging to their mothers, came throngs of more devotees. The musicians, thirsty after hours of playing under the sun, grabbed at paper cups of water handed them by people on the street.

Many people carried burning candles with bases wrapped in foil to protect their hands from the dripping wax. Others, in acts of penitence, walked barefoot upon the scorching asphalt. Some, their eyes moist with tears, murmured soft, private prayers or joined in the ancient chant that spontaneously rose from the center of the crowd:

Evviva Maria   Long live Mary
E chi La Creo   and her Creator.

The scene before us seemed out of place in our times. Still these people weren't performers in some carefully staged reenactment of ancient customs for tourists' cameras. Every emotion displayed was genuine. Nor were they recent arrivals from some distant country, still clinging to their native customs. Second- and third-generation Americans were in the majority. Nor was this peculiar to this town. Variations of the same scene occur throughout the nation wherever Italian populations are concentrated.

To most Italian Americans the *feste,* or feasts, are a natural part of life and require no explanation. But non-Italians are forever mystified by them. Like many components of Italian culture, the feasts rely on the senses to convey their full meaning: to reveal how residential city side streets are transformed once a year into brightly illuminated midways where prayers and hymns somehow mix naturally with the sound of churning carnival ride motors; how stark conflicts between modern Catholicism and stubborn, old traditions are temporarily ignored, and how people work equally hard at piety and pleasure on the same day.

At some point during the sociological cataloguing of ethnic groups, it has been overlooked that Italians are Latins, the original Latins, as the Romans were descendants of the ancient Italic tribe by that name. Italian Americans rarely, if ever, apply the term to themselves, but lingering Latin characteristics remain just the same. Nowhere do they show up more vividly than in the area of religion. The feasts, being religious events, clearly reveal Latin attitudes toward the divine scheme of life.

A chief part of that scheme is the prominent position given to the saints. Saint Bernard, a twelfth-century monk, advised that if you are too timid or ashamed to address your prayers to God, there's always Mary and the saints who will be happy to deliver the message for you. Italians have long subscribed to this philosophy. Italian festivals directly honoring Christ are few. For centuries, Italians have relied on the third-party role of their beloved saints in spiritual affairs.

Some trace the evolution of this arrangement to pre-Christian times. Like most primitive people, the farmers and herdsmen of ancient Italy attributed every natural occurrence or phenomenon to a specific and appropriate deity. Rome's rise to power made it the center of the civilized world and thereby made it vulnerable to the influence of foreign religions. These, too, were bursting at the seams with multitudes of gods and goddesses, many of which were absorbed into the Italic pantheon. By the advent of Christianity, Italians were worshiping a well-populated and varied collection of immortals.

Italy was one of the first European lands to be exposed to Christianity, but the old pagan cults held sway until 312 A.D. That year, while riding into battle, Emperor Constantine saw a vision of the True Cross, and with that, Christianity became the official religion of the land. But its allegiance to one all-powerful God, who was responsible for everything in the universe, was not immediately comprehended by the farmer in the hills who had been accustomed to praying to a certain deity for good crops and an entirely different one to cure his arthritis. As would later happen in other European lands, the developing concept of Christian saints helped fill the void left by the banished pagan gods and served as important agents in the transition to the new religion.

Originally, the saints were simply good Christians who, by leading exemplary lives or through martyrdom, merited an honored memory. Gradually they came to be thought of as able to work wonders and miracles on their own, or at least capable of exercising a little heavenly clout to bring about their occurrence.

Like the old deities, individual saints were given areas of specialty in their powers, always associated with real or legendary events in their earthly lives. Saint Lucy, according to some accounts, had lost an unusually beautiful pair of eyes in the course of her martyrdom. She became the patroness of good vision. Likewise, someone troubled by a sore throat would naturally turn to Saint Blaise for relief, since having once rescued a choking youth from death, he held expertise over that particular anatomical region. If a saint had been a tradesman in life, he would subsequently watch over later practitioners of his craft. Adhering to the basic Christian tenet of monotheism, it was understood, of course, that the saints were still subject to the will of the one Almighty. They were not to be worshiped, but *venerated,* although even that term betrays pagan roots, stemming from the respect paid to the Roman goddess Venus. Folk hero saints, like the fourth century Bishop Paolino of Nola, who rescued citizens of his town from pirates, also became popular in specific cities or regions and inspired civic pride as well as religious devotion, much as Saint Patrick does for the Irish and Joan of Arc for the French.

Given the all-surmounting value placed on the family in Italian culture, it was only natural for the Blessed Mother and Saint Joseph, parent figures of the Holy Family, to be elevated to especially high prominence in the heavenly hierarchy. As the Mother and foster father of Jesus, Mary and Joseph had reliable access to the ear of God and their influence and power were thus second to none.

The roster of saints grew enormously over the centuries and it was considered wise for individuals and whole communities alike to select at least one from the list to serve as guardian of personal or collective welfare. The subsiding of a plague or the repelling of a foreign invasion was thought impossible without the holy patron's intervention. To repay these benevolent actions and to assure their continuation, honoring the saints on their feast days was never neglected. These practices, of course, weren't confined to Italy. By the Middle Ages, cults centering around various saints, and especially around the Blessed Virgin, flourished all across Europe. Besides their uninterrupted retention of such traditions right up to the present, Italians stand out by the unique manner in which they manifest them.

Honoring the saints in a lively festive way evolved both from time-honored, pre-Christian customs and the very attitudes toward the sacred patrons as good and powerful friends. Solemn respect was tempered by the awareness that they too once walked the earth as humans and presumably knew the pains and pleasures of daily life from firsthand experience. Consequently, the relationship between saint and devotee developed into an intensely personal one of human to human with an intimacy that in later days never failed to shock Protestants.

In rural Italian hymns, for instance, Mary is still frequently addressed as "Mamma." And members of the Neapolitan *Parenti*, whose task it is to verbally encourage San Gennaro's dried blood to liquify miraculously on his feast day, can still be heard to harshly scold and rebuke the saint should the "miracle" fail to occur.

As fellow humans, the saints were thought to actually *want* their devotees to have a good time in their honor, and, symbolically at least, even took part in the fun themselves. Music, fireworks, and dazzling street illuminations were developed to high artistry for the enjoyment of those on both sides of the gates of Paradise. Such things bring pleasure and happiness. And happiness, after all, is what Heaven's supposed to be all about.

Prior to the tidal waves of large-scale immigration, Italian Catholicism in America was distinguished mostly by its positive contributions to the propagation of the faith. Courageous Italian missionaries had been penetrating the wilderness of the American continent since the days of Columbus. And a Neapolitan priest, Gennaro de Concilio, in 1873 authored much of the Baltimore Catechism which remained the cornerstone of Catholic religious instruction in American parochial schools for nearly a century.

Severe differences, however, between the generally austere, Irish-dominated American Catholicism and the religious attitudes of southern Italian peasants were readily and glaringly obvious as soon as the latter started pouring through Ellis Island after 1880. Clustering within the insular boundaries of their own urban neighborhoods, these immigrants tenaciously held to their native language and habits, which included the marking of favorite saints' days in the Old Country way. The ranks of Italian clergy in American cities were initially insufficient to serve the ever-growing populations of the various Little Italies, and the churches attended by the immigrants were more often than not administered by Irish priests.

Like most non-Latins, the Irish considered the observing of a religious holiday in such a vibrant and robust fashion to border on outright paganism. The practice was discouraged and even denounced by church pastors.

The effigies of saints, centerpieces of every feast with

their jewel-studded mantles and crowns, brought swift accusations of idolatry from Protestants. Hard-core American nativists, who disliked the immigrants anyway, pointed to the feasts as evidence that Latin culture was at direct odds with old-fashioned Yankee principles. These same people saw nothing scandalous, of course, about the Christmas tree, Yule log, mistletoe, Easter egg, and other symbols of direct pagan derivation that had been worked into their own religious holiday traditions. Thus these important Old World religious festivals survived only through the work of Italian lay immigrants who formed societies that took the responsibility for re-creating the events in the new country.

Through the dedicated labors of Bishop Giovanni Battista Scalabrini's Fathers of Saint Charles, Francesca Cabrini's Missionary Sisters of the Sacred Heart, and other Italian religious orders set up specifically to tend to the immigrants, Italian-administered parishes were gradually established across the United States. With these, Italian-language Masses were lifted out of the church basements where many Irish priests had tried to bury them, and the organization of appropriate feasts by parishioners went unhindered.

The Scalabrini missionaries had an especially profound impact on Italian immigrants to the United States. Having established a religious foundation in Italian-American communities, they began attending to the more social and cultural needs of Italians by setting up social service centers such as schools and homes for the aged, as well as cultural centers and mass communications systems throughout the United States. The mass exodus to the suburbs and the urban renewal programs of the post-World War II decades brought about the disintegration of many old Italian city neighborhoods, but the need for funding and maintaining these important centers provided cause for continued unification among Italian Americans.

It's important to remember that this unification of Italian Americans is a relatively recent phenomenon. The Italian

86

immigrant groups were anything but homogenous. Instead they followed the old *Campanilismo* philosophy that rendered non-Italians and Italians from provinces or regions other than one's own equally foreign and untrustworthy. *Campanilismo* is derived from the Italian word for the village belfry, *campanile.* A Sicilian from a certain town would be as unwilling as he was unwelcome to sit on the committee for a festival honoring a rival Sicilian village's patron saint, much less a Neapolitan or Calabrese one.

Despite this strict regionalism, all feasts generally followed the same pattern. For a week or two, usually in the grueling heat of summer, several crowded, dilapidated blocks of an inner city neighborhood would suddenly find themselves adorned in lights and garlands. The narrow streets were "blanketed" with curb-to-curb canvas by multi-colored booths or tents in close proximity, creating a rainbow or Joseph's coat effect—almost as if it were a gypsy camp.

Tons of spaghetti began to boil and vendors would arrange displays of religious medals, rosaries, scapulars, and statues. At some strategic point of the festival, a brilliantly illuminated bandstand was erected and musicians in crisp uniforms and white gloves provided a constant backdrop of opera, overtures, songs, and triumphant symphonic marches.

The façade of the local church was intricately outlined by thousands of tiny lights, and adjacent to the altar within, the statue of the honored saint was surrounded by fresh flowers and hundreds of burning candles and red vigil lamps. The church doors were kept open for the duration of the festivities as a steady flow of devotees moved in and out. On Sunday, solemn High Mass, sometimes celebrated outdoors to accommodate the crowds, was followed immediately by the procession through the streets with the saint's image held aloft. Even their antagonists had to admit begrudgingly that the Italians showed an uncanny talent for spectacle that surpassed anything other Americans could muster for their own secular festivities.

Treasured Yard Shrines

by Joseph Sciorra

Contemporary Italian Americans continue to give traditional form to their religious beliefs by constructing yard shrines. Stucco chapels, stone grottoes, and brick shrines are built by homeowners to house statues of the Virgin Mary, the Sacred Heart, and a host of Roman Catholic saints. These structures stand in lush rural gardens, concrete urban yards, and on manicured suburban lawns. This public display of religious sentiment has long been a part of the Italian's everyday life.

In Italy's mountain villages and bustling cities, numerous outdoor shrines or *edicole sacre* hold religious images reproduced in paint, tiles, inexpensive prints, and statuettes. One need only remember the opening scene in Puccini's opera, *Tosca*, where Cesare Angelotti recovers a key hidden in a Roman street shrine dedicated to the Madonna, to realize how pervasive this custom is in Italy. In Naples, the popular shrines are constructed in a distinctly baroque style on the sides of public buildings, while in the countryside, simple white chapels stand along the road, looking like scaled-down versions of village churches.

Italian immigrants constructed temporary altars and chapels in the courtyards and on the sidewalks of America's cities as part of their annual religious feasts. The outdoor altar consisted of an ordinary table decorated with a cloth finished in elaborate needlework, atop which were placed numerous candles, flowers, and a print or statue of the saint. Neighbors maintained an all-night vigil at these altars, reciting prayers and singing religious hymns. A large outdoor chapel would be erected by the members of the

88

home-town society responsible for organizing a particular *festa*. The statue of the saint would be kept in such a temporary chapel when it was not being carried in a procession through the neighborhood streets. The tradition of erecting temporary altars and chapels outdoors continues to this day.

When Italian Americans moved out of tenement buildings and into private homes they took full advantage of the American-style front yard. The private yard is a public stage for presenting either horticultural skills and the well-groomed lawn, or religious sentiment and artistic expression, as evidenced by the display of garden statuary, an idea borrowed from Italian garden practices dating from the Renaissance. Yard shrines are not unique to Italian Americans; they are constructed by Catholics of diverse ethnic backgrounds.

The motive for building a shrine in one's yard varies from person to person. Construction of a small chapel is considered by many to be a correct way of honoring a saint. Or a yard shrine may be a memorial to a deceased relative, perhaps with a plaque at the base. Shrines are built in fulfillment of a religious vow made to the Virgin Mary or one of the saints. In most cases a votary petitions for recovery from a serious illness.

Yard shrines are constructed with an array of building materials which range from wood or stone to man-made plastics, fiberglass shingles, and aluminum siding. Leftovers from repair work of house façades and interiors are the bases for many such shrines. A common building material in the United States, difficult to find in Italy, is brick. Found objects such as stones, sea shells, and broken ceramic are often incorporated into the shrine's surface. They are often finished with white paint or stucco. Two common shrine forms are the inverted U-shaped alcove and the pitched roof topped with a cross, replicating a church niche and façade.

A Heritage Recovered

by Fred L. Gardaphe

Many Italian Americans have begun returning to Italy to see the land the immigrants referred to as "the old country." It is an experience that is becoming more common now that Italian Americans have reached a comfortable level of living that makes such travel affordable. It is also a trip that can affect the traveler for the rest of his or her life. This is my story of such a trip.

Grandpa never did fit into what I believed was "American." I grew up thinking that he was just one of those interesting characters of the past who was out of place in the world of astronauts and television. Grandpa was an immigrant who had never really arrived, one who carried the burlap sack of his past wherever he went, a weight that slowed him down in fast-moving, modern America. He seemed to have his own world that had more to do with Italy than America. Whatever image of Italy I held in my youth came from him. He reflected a dual image of my Italian heritage: one of pride and one of embarrassment. These two images constantly fought one another. When I could only see him as the immigrant, Italy remained strange and

Fred L. Gardaphe and son Frederico

foreign. But when I was close to him, I was close to Italy and could see the man behind the immigrant.

I was always embarrassed by his mixture of Italian and English. His broken English upset me, especially when he would "speaka like-a thisa" to me while I was with my non-Italian-American friends, the ones he'd call "mericans." I was always enchanted by his Italian, that strange tongue he would use when spurred to a highly emotional point in an argument, while reminiscing with old friends, or when he didn't want us to understand what he was saying. His language was only one of his ways that was in conflict with the America I was growing up in.

I remember coming down from my bedroom one morning for breakfast, seeing him hunched over a ceramic bowl filled with hunks of stale bread, the kind Mrs. Rossi used to throw out to the birds in her back yard. I watched in disbelief as he poured hot coffee over the bread and then added scalded milk and sugar to the mixture. Then he ate it!

While he was eating I gathered the courage to spill some cornflakes into my blue plastic bowl and eat the American breakfast I knew from television. He offered me a taste of his concoction, which I rudely refused, to his amusement. When I looked into his smile I lost the image I had had of him when I first saw him pour the coffee over the old bread. In that closeness I loved, but didn't understand, the immigrant.

Grandpa never used the products I thought were essential to American life. He bragged that he had never used shampoo or toothpaste and yet managed to keep a full head of beautiful hair and a mouth free of fillings. I was amazed, since by the age of ten I was already noticing dandruff and had visited the dentist more than he ever had in all his seventy years of life. He preferred to grow his own vegetables while I'd be fascinated by the ease of picking unblemished, even-sized tomatoes and other produce neatly wrapped in plastic off supermarket shelves. I was frustrated by the hours I would spend with him in his garden, sweating to produce a few tomatoes and peppers, or following him through fields of forest preserves picking dandelion greens and poking puffballs down from trees.

Grandma was always the center of attention during the preparation of Sunday afternoon meals. She ruled the kitchen and hollered out orders to the women in our family. But my attention always turned to Grandpa while we ate.

He fascinated me, using bread in fingers to gather sauce that slid off the spaghetti, tonguing neckbones until they were meatless and dry. He could make me forget I had food in front of me; he was a noisy eater, but the sounds he made were hardly noticeable amid the loud talk at the table. He rationed the salad of bitter dandelion greens by dancing around the table and dropping them onto plates, then would return to his seat, hug the huge wooden bowl with one arm and shovel forkfuls of greens into his mouth. When the storm of the meal had blown over, he would sit back and smoke an unfiltered cigarette, often for effect, with the lit end in his mouth. Magic! we used to think.

Grandpa never learned to read or write and I would feel so important when he would ask me to read something to him. I was the American he could never be. I was proof that his hopes of "making it" in America had been fulfilled.

In World War I Italy decreed that if the immigrants of military service age did not come home to serve in the Italian army, they could not come back to see relatives for 40 years. Grandpa went back in 1918 to serve in the army, and returned to America in 1921. Grandpa never told me why he originally left Italy, and never talked of his childhood. After he died, Sunday dinners were never the same. With him were buried many of the Italian traditions our family had followed at his lead. Without his influence, Italians became strangers to me, a collage of media images: spicy meatball eaters, Godfather types, and opera buffoons. But Grandpa did leave me with a curiosity about what the "old country" was like.

*Left: The Feast of Saint Rosalia,
Boston, Massachusetts.*
—Photographs by Harry Oster
*Right: The Feast of Maria S. S.
Lauretana, Berwyn, Illinois.*
—Photographs by Joan Liffring-Zug

Virginia Basso Wheatley is shown in her store, Providence Cheese and Tavola (hot table), one of the quaint shops in the Italian neighborhood of Federal Hill, Providence, Rhode Island. Inside the store is this sign: "Welcome back to the 19th Century." Note bread dough sculptures in photo.

84

to find work in America. The plan was for him to make enough money for the family to buy the land they worked from the Don (landlord) who owned it. He would send money back to Castellana and promised in each letter that one day he would return. That one day did not come, for soon he had a family of his own to support.

Learning all this helped me to regain a part of me that was lost when he died. I was whole, and proud now more than ever of my Italian heritage. My pride no longer stemmed from ignorance. It was a pride of wisdom and of love for the sacrifices he had made to give his descendants life in America.

Each day in Castellana began with a breakfast of hard bread in a ceramic bowl over which I poured coffee, scalded milk and sugar. I had to laugh at myself as I recalled that morning, so many years earlier, when I saw Grandpa eating the same. I visited the house where Grandpa was born and spent a long time inside the stone cottage, touching what he had once touched, seeing what he had seen. I was so lost in emotion I cried without trying to hide my tears. I felt this place had some kind of power over me. When I left his home, I felt for the first time that I had a history, a history I had never studied in school, a history that would have remained lost had I not traveled to Castellana Grotte.

I spent my last day in Italy in Monopoli. Alone, I sat on the beach, staring into the sun's reflection on the rolling waves. I realized that I was seeing what Grandpa had been staring at that day years ago on the beach in southern California and I thought, "Someday I will come back to Castellana." Little did I know then that a few years later I would be married in Castellana, but that's another story. Right, Grandpa?

Italian Cuisine

by Miriam Canter

Candelaus are decorative almond cookies molded by hand in Sardinia in the shape of boots, baskets, or slippers.

The cuisine of Italy is really the cooking of its many regions, each quite distinct because of historical and geographical differences. Each area was a separate political entity until 1861, when Italy was united under Emmanuel II.

Much of what is considered French cuisine is actually derived from Italian foods. When Catherine de' Medici left Florence in 1533 to become the bride of the Duke of Orleans, she took with her a bevy of Italian cooks and many utensils, such as the fork, which were unknown in France. Especially fond of sweets and desserts, she introduced some marvelous concoctions known today as French pastries. The duke, as King Henry II, ruled France from 1547 to 1559. Three of their four sons became French kings.

Marco Polo and other Italian traders brought back exotic foods and spices from the Orient and the Middle East. Columbus and other explorers brought back from the New World tomatoes, corn, potatoes, and cocoa, all of which were incorporated into the Italian cuisine, depending in part upon where they could be grown. In the North rice and corn grew easily, while in the South it was tomatoes and olives. Spices and wines were everywhere.

Despite the historical traditions of regional foods, a trend toward more uniformity in the foods of Italy is being caused by modern transportation and communication. Fresh fish can be found in the inland and mountain areas while the rice and corn dishes show up on the coasts. Nevertheless, each region continues to be identified with its traditional foods, and the shapes of the pastas, the sauces and the toppings can identify their origin. Areas no more than 50 miles apart may feature a different food or style of preparation as well as different traditions.

Butter for frying, soft egg pasta, and veal are found in the North, to be replaced by olive oil, dried pastas, and beef in the South. The two northernmost regions, Piedmont and Lombardy, share the rich Po River valley. Most of Italy's rice, corn, cattle and dairy products are produced there. Italy is the largest producer of rice in Europe. Milan, the major city of the North, has developed a well-known style of cooking using saffron. Many such dishes, popular the world over, are designated *alla Milanese.* Dishes of rice, *risotto,* and cornmeal *polenta* are common everyday fare. *Bagna cauda* from Turin is an anchovy fondue with assorted vegetables used as dippers. Many kinds of fruits are produced in this region, and the wines are red and dry. Mushrooms and truffles are used in abundance. Specialties found in other cities of this area are spit-roasted birds in Bergamo, frogs in Pavia, and many kinds of sausages. The cities along the lakes and rivers offer trout, eels and salmon. The world-famous *panettone,* a colorful Christmas bread, is said to have originated in Milan.

Southwest of this area is Liguria, where the mild climate produces a wide range of herbs. Although this area borders the sea, fish are not plentiful. One very elaborate fish dish, *cappon magro,* comes from Genoa. It is made of several layers of fish, shaped into a pyramid, served with an anchovy sauce, and presented on a highly decorated plate. Stuffed vegetables are common and veal is the popular meat. Liguria is best known for the basil and oil sauce, *pesto,* which has become a favorite in this country too, especially over pasta. The Ligurians developed candied fruits which are used in many pastries such as *pandolce,* a holiday specialty. It is also said that the Genovese invented ravioli.

East of Lombardy and bordering the Adriatic Sea is Veneto. Its most famous city, Venice, is known for its canals, bridges, and unexcelled cuisine. Spices, reflecting the effect of early Oriental traders, are in great supply, providing stronger flavors than are found in other areas. Veneto has a wonderful variety of fish and seafood as well as grains. Cornmeal dishes are popular, beginning with the everyday dish *polenta,* similar to our cornmeal mush. Rice is prepared in countless ways with sauces made from vegetables, meats and fish. Sea bass, eel, cuttlefish, sole, and shellfish such as oysters, crabs and snails, together with lamb, goat, and fowl make up a large part of the diet. A unique dish is *bisato sull' ara* made of eel sautéed with laurel leaves. Special cheeses such as *asiago* and *montasio* as well as caramelized dried fruits appear at the end of meals. Venetian wines tend to be light and delicate, ideal served with the seafood and white meats that are typically eaten here. *Risi e bisi,* rice with peas, originated here but is now an international dish. *Radicchio,* a purple variety of chicory, is a beautiful plant that now dresses up countless salads in this country. Verona, another city in Veneto with a glorious history in the arts, is also known for its own famous egg pasta, *gnocchi,* resembling tiny dumplings. Venetians make their own form of *pesto* sauce, and one will find basil growing everywhere, from gardens to small pots on window ledges.

The incredibly lush plains of Emilia-Romagna are responsible for agricultural products of great quantity and quality. Most of Italy's wheat is grown here and the vegetables and fruits are among the best in the country. The Adriatic Sea, refreshed by water from the mountain rivers, supplies the most delicate varieties of fish. While pork and veal are the choice meats, cured hams and sausages of all kinds are typical of this area. Indeed, its most famous city, Bologna, gave its name to what has become a ubiquitous product. Another city, Parma, is said to have developed Parmesan cheese, popular all over the world. Its production here is strictly controlled, with rulings over such details as the kind of cows that provide the milk and the narrow range of time during which it can be made, i.e., between April 1 and November 11 of each year. Two other provinces, Reggio and Piacenza, also claim this cheese. A savory meat and vegetable sauce, *ragù,* was invented in Bologna. *Tortellini,* little stuffed pockets of dough, are also Bolognese, but now almost every province has its own version based on different kinds of stuffings. Some of Italy's best red wines come from this region although most other types are found to go with a variety of foods.

South of Emilia, between the mountains and the sea on Italy's western coast, is Tuscany, whose lovely city, Florence, has also provided a style named for itself, *alla Fiorentina,* in the Florentine manner. In the United States this usually refers to a dish served with spinach. In Florence, however, it usually implies a simple presentation with a salad, such as the classic *bistecca alla Fiorentina,* a plain grilled steak, brushed with the finest olive oil. Simplicity is the key word in Tuscan cooking, with meats and fish prepared primarily on a grill or over an open fire, seasoned with herbs but served without sauces. Many restaurants, called *girarrosto,* are so-called because they feature spit-roasted meats and poultry. The land here is not very fertile but is ideal for olive trees. Lucca is the center of olive oil production and the finest is shipped all over the world. Other specialties of this area include a sort of fish stew, *cacciucco,* and *panforte,* a wonderful Christmas cake made from nuts, cocoa, fruits, and spices. *Chianti* is one of the famed Tuscan wines as well as *vinsanto,* a strong, sweet wine used for holy occasions.

South of Tuscany, hugging the coastline, is Latium with Rome as its major city. As the nation's capital with its highly civilized history, its cuisine is sophisticated and eclectic. The quantity and colorful presentation of food hints at the orgies of long ago. Suckling lamb, kid, and young pigs are traditional meats. Fish and vegetables are common and are treated in many ways. Artichokes are very popular, and are made *alla giudia,* whose name conveys its Jewish origins. Rome's most famous pasta dish is *spaghetti all' amatriciana,* with its sauce made from tomatoes, peppers, onions, and salt pork. Dry white wines and dessert pastries made with ricotta cheese are typical.

East of the mountains are a number of smaller regions with cuisines that vary in subtle ways. The Marches and Umbria compete in wine production. Landlocked Umbria gets its seafood from the coastal areas, especially from Abruzzi, whose rocky soil is not suitable for extensive vineyards. Abruzzi grows saffron and provides this spice to much of the world. In Abruzzi, some liqueurs are flavored with saffron.

Campania becomes truly southern Italy. Warm sunny days produce wonderful vegetables, especially the prolific tomato that came to the area in the sixteenth century and is the mainstay of most dishes. Naples is the major city, and Neapolitan food seems to represent Italian cuisine the world over. Pizza, spaghetti, and many other forms of pasta are very popular. The modern Italians prefer to buy their pasta, while in the United States use of the homemade variety is increasing because of the many pasta-making machines now available. The sauces are as varied as the shapes of the pasta, but they all have a tomato base. Perhaps the most famous pizza is *pizza Margherita,* named for the first queen of Italy. It is a patriotic dish with its topping made of red tomatoes, white mozzarella cheese, and green basil, the colors of the Italian flag. Fish is more common than red meat, and cheeses and wines are in good supply. Some of the grape varieties and methods of wine-making date from ancient Rome.

Basilicata, south of Campania and north of Calabria, is known for sausages. *Baccalà* (codfish) and other salted and smoked fish are popular.

Calabria, the toe of Italy's boot shape, has many shepherds who produce a variety of cheeses. In fertile spots are olive groves and flower plantations. Sausages, primarily of pork, are made in great variety. Some fruits and nuts are grown, dried, and shipped all over the world. Calabrian figs are a delicacy everywhere. Calabrians bake lots of bread, some huge 20-pound loaves, often flavored with such ingredients as tomatoes, herbs, and even sardines. The wines of this area are heavier than elsewhere and make a good balance for the spicy foods.

Wheat and vegetables are grown in Puglia, the heel of Italy's boot. The variety of seafood available there is astounding, but cooking styles are simple. Puglia is famed for its ear-shaped pasta called *orecchietti*. Wines of Puglia are heavy, have a high alcoholic content, and are often used for blending with other Italian wines.

Across the Strait of Messina lies the island of Sicily. Its climate is intensely hot, but literally tons of fruits and vegetables survive the burning sun, and Sicily provides much of Europe with citrus fruits. Basic Sicilian cooking relies on tomatoes, olive oil, fresh tuna and swordfish, sardines, pork, and various pastas. Spaghetti cooked with squid in their own ink is a specialty. Butter is not used at all for cooking. What milk is available is used for cheese. Grapes grow well in Sicily, and *Marsala,* a world-famous wine, is made in the city of that name.

Marsala is also known for a dish called *couscous,* which originated in North Africa. The Italian version is made of *semolina* (a heavier, grainy flour) mixed with water and formed into tiny beads. These are then combined with a rich fish broth, chopped garlic, and some olive oil and steamed over the fish broth. The finished dish is eaten with the addition of more fish broth and fish.

Rice, nuts, and other grains are omens of fertility and good wishes. With this in mind, many families in Palermo serve stuffed rice balls called *arancini* (little oranges) at weddings, baptisms, and other occasions. On the feast of Saint Lucia, when no bread or other wheat items are eaten, some families prepare a dish called *riso 'n cascito*. It is a casserole of rice, sautéed cauliflower, meat sauce and cheese. Pastries are popular, often made with the fine Sicilian fruits and nuts, as well as the local ricotta cheese. Ice cream, *gelato*, was discovered by the French when they invaded Sicily in the seventeenth century. Popular in Roman times was *granita*, shaved ice flavored with lemon or coffee; in those days the ice came from the mountains.

Sardinia *(Sardegna)*, an island off the west coast of Italy, attracts tourists and prosperity with its San Francisco-like climate, its ocean fishing, some of the most exclusive and expensive resorts in Europe, and fine restaurants. A nude beach in Sardinia was Europe's first. Some Sardinian specialties: *Gnocchi Sardi*, tiny dumplings made by hand in the form of an elongated seashell; *candelaus*, small almond paste cookies in the shape of slippers, boots, baskets, et cetera, decorated with icing, silver paper, and silvered candy balls; and *couscous*, common here as in Marsala.

Typical Menus

A typical dinner menu, whether in an Italian home or a restaurant, begins with the appetizers, *antipasti*. These may be as simple as an assortment of fruits with the thinly sliced ham we know as *prosciutto* (in Sardinia it is made with wild boar) or as elaborate as a large tray of pickled vegetables, several kinds of cured meats or salamis, olives, and small shellfish. The first course, or *primo piatto*, may be a soup, a pasta, risotto, occasionally a fish dish, or a combination of any of these. The pastas may be served with a simple sauce or incorporated into a more satisfying dish with meats and cheeses. The second course, *secondo piatto*, is the main course of meat, fish, or eggs. The best beef is found in Tuscany, but veal and other young animals are more common. Much of the pork is cured. Fish include trout, halibut, sea bass, and snapper. Squid, cuttlefish, eel, and many varieties of shrimp, clams and lobsters are typical Italian seafoods that are not commonly served in the United States. The *frittata,* a delicious egg omelet, is often served as a light lunch. It is made with chopped vegetables. Salads and vegetables are served with or following the second course. Vegetables, *verdure,* are usually boiled, then lightly sautéed with butter or olive oil and Parmesan cheese. Artichokes, eggplant, broccoli and spinach are among the favorites. Salads, *insalate,* may be an assortment of fresh greens, dressed in olive oil and wine vinegar poured on in order, not mixed together. This is always served after the second course. Another type of salad, made with cold cooked meats or fish, and often mixed with rice and raw or cooked vegetables, may be served as an antipasto, a first or second course, but never as the salad course. Following the salad, cheeses and fruits are usually the final course. Parmesan and gorgonzola are especially good with fresh ripe fruits. Sweet desserts and pastries are generally served for special occasions such as holidays or family celebrations. Wines are served with every course and vary according to the kind of dish served.

Festival Foods

Capo d' Anno—New Year's: Some families serve an elaborate meal just before midnight while others wait until the Day itself. The main course might be the traditional roast suckling pig served with crackling brown artichokes. This would be an occasion for a very special dessert, perhaps a *torta di ricotta,* a cheese pie. Adults sometimes exchange gifts, and the merrymaking might last into the night.

Festa di San Giuseppe—Saint Joseph's Day: This occurs on March 19 and honors the patron saint of home and family. It is celebrated by rich and poor alike and begins with a religious celebration. The rich invite the poor to eat, and often a public buffet banquet takes place in the village square. No cheese is eaten on this holy day and pasta may be sprinkled with a mixture of toasted dry crumbs, fresh sardines and fennel sauce. Lentils and other dried beans are served, all without cheese. The traditional dessert is *Bignè di San Giuseppe,* a large round pastry resembling a cream puff, filled with pastry cream and dusted with powdered sugar or topped with fruit.

Carnevale — Carnival: This occurs during the four weeks preceding Lent, and is the merriest holiday of the year. The last part of the festival, called "The Two Days of the Shepherds," is the time for most of the celebration. As always, food plays an important part in the event. One traditional dish, *salsiccia con peperoni,* is made of broiled sausage and sautéed green peppers. The sausage is highly seasoned with Caciocavallo cheese, chopped parsley and fennel seed.

Pasqua—Easter: Breakfast usually features eggs prepared with vegetables and herbs. The festive meat is typically a roasted baby lamb served with artichokes roasted to a golden brown. Holiday breads in many shapes and designs are often baked with eggs hidden inside. Sometimes a large bread shaped in a ring is placed on the dinner table, surrounded by colored eggs. Desserts may be an assortment of cookies with ice cream or with cream tarts, *cassatelle.*

Natale—Christmas: A traditional supper is generally served late on Christmas Eve, before the family goes to midnight Mass. No meat is served, only fish, and *capitone,* large eels, are often the choice. Soup with some sort of pasta and little cream tarts make up the meal. On Christmas Day, *Natale,* dinner is a veritable feast. Roast suckling pig, baby lamb, or whole chickens are typical. More desserts are served than at any other time. They may include cookies, tortes, fruits, and nuts, elaborately presented.

At festive meals *caffè espresso* (strong coffee) is served at the end and wines are served throughout the meal, chosen to complement the dishes they accompany. Despite regional specialties and family preferences, some holiday foods are basic and are present in some form throughout Italy.

Basic Ingredients
for Italian-American Cooks

Rice
Grown in northern regions, the *arborio* variety is short and thick-grained, unlike American types. Water is continually added as it cooks, resulting in a creamy product.

Cheese
Parmigiano-Reggiano, one of the finest, is used in pastas and soups, and with fruits. *Gorgonzola* is a blue-veined cheese used in sauces and as a table cheese. Traditionally, *mozzarella* is made from the milk of water buffalo, but it is also made from that of cows. *Ricotta* is a fresh soft-curd cheese made much as cottage cheese is. It is used in desserts and on pastas and is very perishable. *Pecorino* is made from sheep's milk. The best comes from Tuscany although one variety, *Romano* from Rome, which hardens as it ages, is used grated over pasta dishes. *Fontina* is a buttery cheese made in the Piedmont region. One type is made in summer and one in winter.

Herbs
Most commonly used are basil, rosemary, sage, oregano, fennel, garlic, and parsley. Basil is the most popular in the North. Oregano spices up southern tomato sauces.

Olive Oil
Extra virgin is made from underripe olives and is pressed only once. Virgin is made from slightly riper olives and also is pressed just once. Pure olive oil is the most common and is processed by chemical means. The flavors are stronger and the acidity higher as the grade declines.

Wines
The varieties are as infinite as are the varieties of grapes. Climatic and topographical conditions account for flavor

variations even within a kind of wine. The best known wines are Marsala, Chianti, Valpolicella, Soave, and Frascati. Wine production is one of the largest industries in Italy, with hundreds of tiny wineries.

Vegetables and Fruits

Tomatoes, eggplant, zucchini, beans, asparagus, artichokes, onions, peppers, and spinach are the most common vegetables. They are cooked in sauces, pickled, or tossed and served with an oil-vinegar dressing. Oranges, apples, cherries, peaches, grapes, figs, and all kinds of berries are usually eaten raw with cheese at the end of a meal.

Fish

Many varieties also found in the New World are here, such as cod, tuna, sole, swordfish, and perch, as well as cuttlefish, squid, eel, and all manner of shellfish. Ocean, lakes and rivers provide great variety. Methods of preparation vary from simple sautéeing to elaborate combinations of fish with vegetables or pastas.

Meats

Some beef is available, but it is generally expensive as Italy does not have wide areas for raising cattle. The young animals of all kinds are more commonly eaten, such as lamb, kid, and pigs. Poultry is also common. Pork is often made into cured hams or into many kinds of sausages.

Breads

The individuality of the bakers as well as regional traditions accounts for the more than 1,000 different breads known to the Italians. Some are soft, some crusty, some even baked twice and dried in order to last a long time. Some breads are baked only for special occasions, religious holidays, or family celebrations. They may be simple loaves in special shapes, or baked with such ingredients as spices, fruits, nuts, eggs, and milk.

Pizzas

Pizza, as it is called in southern Italy, or *Focaccia* in the North, is a flat round bread. It probably developed from a leftover piece of dough but has become a common dish topped with oil, tomatoes, and cheese, known especially in the Neapolitan area, and eaten primarily as a snack. In World War II, American GIs discovered this delight while serving in Italy. After the war, they created the demand for pizza in this country, resulting in the many American-style pizzerias. Crusts, thick or thin, are piled high with every kind of vegetable, meat, and cheese. True to Italian tradition, we are even developing regional styles such as Chicago pizza.

Pasta

Pasta is the main symbol of Italian food today. Its origins can be traced to the Roman Empire, long before Marco Polo brought noodles back from China. It is a simple food, made of flour, water, eggs (sometimes not), and occasionally chopped spinach or tomato paste for subtle color and flavor. The dough is rolled out very thin, cut into various shapes by hand or pasta machine, cooked fresh or, more commonly, dried and stored for future use. To cook pasta one needs only to boil it until it is *al dente* or tender but firm to the bite. Pasta is found in appetizers, main dishes, and side dishes, as well as desserts. Pasta dishes have become increasingly popular in the United States, due in part to the ease of preparation, and also because they have become part of the health food craze. Pasta is made from hard, high-protein wheat, and nutritionists recommend it for its food value and relatively low calorie count.

Pastas are divided into two classes, those that are to be filled or stuffed and those that are not. The former includes *ravioli, lasagne, tortellini,* and *cannelloni,* which are filled with meats, cheeses, or vegetables, baked in or served with a sauce. The second category includes all varieties of noodles, spaghetti, *maccheroni, rigatoni,* and *fettuccine.* They vary in thickness and width, the thinnest, *tagliatelle,* measuring less than a millimeter. There are countless shapes, many of which are regionally traditional.

Soups, Salads & Sauces

Una cena senza vino è come una famiglia senza figli."
"A dinner without wine is like a family without children."
—Amadeo Yelmini

Lentil and Italian Sauce Soup
Zuppa di Lenticchie e Salsiccia

Josephine Scalissi Grunewald
Blairstown, Iowa

"My parents emigrated to America from Piana De Greci, Sicily in 1902, arriving in New Orleans. Piana De Greci was a 16th century Albanian settlement. They raised their family of 11 children in Madison, Wisconsin."

1 1/2 cups lentils
7 cups water
1/4 cup spinach, fresh or frozen
1 tablespoon salt
1/2 teaspoon black pepper
1 tablespoon basil
1/4 cup diced celery
1/4 cup diced onions
2 carrots, diced or sliced thin
1/2 pound ham, cubed
6 Italian sausage links, cooked

Rinse the lentils and place them in a large kettle with the water, spinach, seasonings, vegetables and ham. Cover and boil gently for 2 hours. Cut the links into 1/4-inch slices and add to the soup. Cook 10 minutes longer. Lentil soup traditionally is a thick hearty potage. Thin with water if you prefer. Sherry or Italian wine can be added to taste. Serve hot. Makes 3 quarts.

Fennel Soup with Fish Broth
Zuppa di Pesci con Finocchio

Ippolito Cavalcanti
Duke of Buonvicino
Naples, Italy, 1837

one bunch wild fennel
1/2 teaspoon salt
5 tablespoons olive oil
1 cup diced onion
2 tablespoons chopped fresh parsley
4 salted anchovies, rinsed
2 1/2 cups fish stock
freshly ground pepper to taste
seasoned croutons

Chop the fennel. Place it in a pan and add water just to cover. Add the salt and cook until tender. Sauté the onion, parsley and anchovies in the oil. Heat the fish stock just to boiling and add the onion mixture. Reduce heat and simmer 20 minutes. Drain the fennel and add it to the fish stock. Season to taste. Serves 4.

Italian Vegetable Soup
Minestrone

Mary Pucci Couchman, M.D.
Rockport, Massachusetts

There is an old Tuscan adage that succinctly tells the Italian philosophy on eating: "A tavola non ci s' invecchia mai." Translation: "At the table, we never grow old."

4 to 5 tablespoons olive oil
3 potatoes, diced or cubed
2 carrots, diced
2 onions, diced
2 cloves garlic, diced
3 stalks celery, diced
2 to 3 sprigs parsley
2 to 3 quarts of beef stock
Italian seasonings
1 28-ounce can Italian tomatoes
1 10-ounce package frozen mixed
   vegetables
2 cups cubed lean pork
2 cups shredded cabbage
2 cups cooked elbow shaped
   pasta, drained
Parmesan cheese

Sauté the potatoes, carrots, onions, garlic, celery, and parsley in the olive oil. When partially cooked add the beef stock. Season to taste with Italian seasonings. Add the tomatoes, frozen vegetables, and pork. Simmer 10 minutes. Add the cabbage. Cook about 15 minutes. Add the pasta. Serve garnished with Parmesan cheese. Pass the Italian bread. This is great fare for a cold winter day. Its flavor improves the next day. Serves 8 to 10.

Opposite: California wines from Italian-American vineyards.

Tortellini Soup
Brodo con Tortellini

Rene Pagliai
Iowa City, Iowa

This recipe is from Rene's mother-in-law Catrina Pagliai who came to America in 1914. Catrina settled with her husband in Zookspur, Iowa, a coal mining camp.

Filling:
1 pound chicken breast
1/4 pound beef steak
1 teaspoon nutmeg
3 eggs
1 cup grated Parmesan cheese
salt and pepper

Dough:
2 cups flour
3 eggs
1 tablespoon oil
3/4 teaspoon salt

Soup:
4 quarts chicken broth
1 quart beef broth

Filling: Boil the chicken and beef until tender. Cool and put through a grinder or chop in a food processor. Add the nutmeg, eggs, cheese, and salt and pepper to taste.
Dough: Place all the ingredients in a food processor and mix until the dough becomes a ball. Cover with a damp cloth and let rest 1/2 hour. Makes 1/2 pound. Roll the dough out thin. Cut the dough into 2 1/2x3-inch rectangles. Place about 1/2 teaspoon of filling onto each rectangle and fold to seal.
Soup: Bring the chicken and beef broth to a boil. Cook the tortellini in the broth until done. Makes 1 1/2 gallons.

Pasta with Zucchini
Pasta con Zucchini

Ann Sorrentino
Hinsdale, Illinois

6 small or 4 large zucchini
1 medium-sized onion
2 cloves garlic
1/3 cup olive oil
1 small piece of hard Romano or
   Parmesan cheese, optional
2 large basil leaves or
   1/2 teaspoon dried basil
3 fresh mint leaves or
   1/2 teaspoon dried mint
2 tablespoons chopped fresh or
   1 teaspoon dried parsley
2 cups tomatoes, canned or fresh,
   puréed
1/4 teaspoon oregano
salt and pepper to taste
1/2 teaspoon sugar
1 cup pasta, *ditalini* or *linguini*
Romano or Parmesan cheese,
   grated

Scrape the zucchini very lightly. Wash, dice, and set aside. Dice the onion and mince the garlic. Heat the oil, add the onion, and cook about 5 minutes over medium heat. Add the garlic and cheese, if used, and sauté another 5 minutes or so. Add the tomatoes, spices, and sugar. Cook for about 10 minutes breaking down tomato fibers with a fork. Add the diced zucchini and cook 10 minutes, stirring occasionally. Add the water to make a soupy mixture. Cook either 1 cup *ditalini* (small tubular pasta) or *linguini* broken into 1-inch pieces in boiling salted water for about 5 minutes. Drain and add to the boiling soup mixture. Continue cooking another 8 to 10 minutes. Check for seasoning, remove the piece of cheese, if used, and serve at once in soup bowls, sprinkling generously with grated cheese. You may prefer to omit the piece of cheese in cooking, in which case you may stir in 2 tablespoons of grated cheese just before serving. Serves 4 to 6.

A SALUTE TO CONGRESSMAN FRANK ANNUNZIO

Ann Sorrentino, left, is in the costume of Palermo, Sicily. Her niece Marie Massicotta wears a costume from Venezia Giulia, her daughter Anne Marie wears the Abruzzi region attire and son Joey wears the garb of Palio de Siena. They are on a float in the Chicago Columbus Day Parade.

Italian Olive Relish
Condimento di Olive

Marie Gattuso
Jefferson Auxiliary of
Italian-American Society
New Orleans, Louisiana

1 quart (32-ounce jar) broken
   green olives
1 cup celery, cut in 1/4-inch to
   1/2-inch pieces
1 medium-sized onion, chopped
1 carrot, cut into 1/4-inch pieces
4 to 6 cloves garlic, minced
2 tablespoons capers, drained
2 teaspoons oregano
juice of 1 lemon
rind of 1/2 lemon, cut in small pieces
1/4 cup olive oil
1/4 cup white vinegar
black pepper to taste

Drain and wash the broken olives
thoroughly; this is very important.
Clean and reserve the jar. Cut the
large olives into 8 pieces, small olives into 4 pieces. In a large mixing
bowl, place all the ingredients and
mix thoroughly. Return to the
cleaned olive jar and place the remaining olive relish in any clean jar;
never store in plastic containers.
Marinate overnight before serving.
If family members permit, the Italian
Olive Relish will remain in the refrigerator in a tightly sealed glass jar for
2 to 3 months. Always serve at
room temperature. Makes 1 quart.
   Use as an appetizer with crackers
or Italian bread, as a salad with
mixed greens or crab, as a relish.
Use on sandwiches or pizza.

Mushroom Salad
Insalata di Funghi

The Honorable Richard F. Celeste
Governor of Ohio
Columbus, Ohio

3 (12-ounce) boxes of mushrooms
2 bunches parsley
1 clove garlic
4 tablespoons olive oil
4 tablespoons wine vinegar
juice of 1 fresh lemon
salt and pepper to taste

Slice the mushrooms thickly and
put them in a large salad bowl. Chop
the parsley; thinly slice the garlic,
and add to the bowl. Add the olive
oil, vinegar, lemon juice, salt, and
pepper. Toss lightly before serving.
Serves 12.

Fennel Salad
Insalata di Finocchio

Josephine Scalissi Grunewald

1 head iceberg lettuce
2 stalks fennel, chopped
leaves from one bunch fennel,
   chopped
2 1/2 cups fresh beets, cooked and
   sliced
1/3 cup olive oil
3 tablespoons wine vinegar
salt and freshly ground pepper

Remove the core and wash the lettuce with cold water. Drain. When
dry, cut or tear into bite-sized pieces
and mix them with the fennel stalks
and leaves. Just before serving add
the beets, oil, vinegar, and salt and
pepper to taste. Toss until the ingredients and dressing are blended.
Serves 6.

Seafood Salad
Insalata con Pesci di Mare

Anna Cesario
Norridge, Illinois

This is the salad shown in the jar Anna is holding in the photograph on the back cover.

1 pound octopus, cleaned
1 pound shrimp, cleaned
1 lemon, sliced
10 bay leaves
1 pound *calamari*, cleaned
1 cup lemon juice
10 cloves garlic, minced
1 cup finely chopped celery
1/2 cup finely chopped parsley
12 1/2-ounce jar of *Giardiniera*,
    a mix of pickled vegetables*
1/2 cup sweet red peppers, cut
    into 1/4-inch cubes
2 tablespoons ground black pepper
1 tablespoon black peppercorns
white vinegar
3/4 cup 100% virgin olive oil

In boiling salted water cook the octopus by holding the head and dunking the legs in 3 to 4 times. When the legs are curled up drop the whole octopus in and boil for 15 minutes. Place the shrimp, lemon slices and bay leaves in a pot of cold water, bring to a boil and cook for 7 to 8 minutes. Remove from heat, drain, and remove the bay leaves. Boil the *calamari* separately for 15 minutes. With a scissors or knife cut the seafood into rings, thicker than a finger. Combine the seafood, lemon juice, garlic, celery, parsley, *Giardiniera*, sweet red peppers, and black pepper. Cover all of this with white vinegar. Allow to marinate for 1 day. Or, to preserve, cover with vinegar for 1 week. To serve, drain off the lemon juice and vinegar; add the 100% virgin olive oil. As an appetizer it serves 8 to 10 people.

Giardiniera is a mixture of finely chopped turnips, carrots, cauliflower, celery, peppers, gherkins, onions, fennel, salt, sugar, and wine vinegar. It can be purchased in many grocery stores in Italian-American neighborhoods.

Italian Salad
Insalata Italiana

Rene Pagliai

This salad is delicious served with crusty bread and red wine.

1 large red onion, sliced
2 medium-sized cucumbers, peeled
    and cut into chunks
6 medium-sized tomatoes, cubed
2 large green peppers, sliced
salt and pepper to taste

Dressing:
3/4 cup olive oil
1/3 cup vinegar
2 tablespoons chopped fresh
    parsley
1 teaspoon dried basil
garlic to taste

Dressing: Blend all the ingredients.
Salad: Place the vegetables in the dressing and marinate at least 4 hours. Serves 6.

Opposite: Piazza d' Italia, 1979 Architectural Design winner. New Orleans, Louisiana.

Lemon and Oil Salad Dressing

*Condimento di Limone
ed Olio per Insalata*

Ann Sorrentino

1/2 cup fresh lemon juice
   (2 to 3 lemons)
1 large clove garlic, mashed
1 tablespoon chopped fresh
   parsley or 1 teaspoon
   dried parsley
1/2 teaspoon oregano, or to taste
1/2 teaspoon basil, or to taste
1 teaspoon onion salt
1 teaspoon salt
2 fresh mint leaves, chopped
1/2 teaspoon Worcestershire
   sauce
1/2 teaspoon freshly ground pepper
3/4 cup olive oil

Put the lemon juice in a bowl and add all the ingredients except the oil. Mix and stir to dissolve the salts. Add the oil, slowly beating into the juice mixture. If it is not to be used immediately, store it in a tightly covered jar in the refrigerator. Shake well before using.

This is good on all fish salads, vegetables, and boiled meat from soup. It is an excellent Sicilian marinade for chicken, fish, and chops in preparation for either baking or broiling. Makes 1 1/2 cups.

Vegetable Appetizer

Antipasto

*I Campagnoli Folk Dancers
Pittsburgh, Pennsylvania*

1/2 head cauliflower, broken into
   small pieces
2 carrots, halved and cut into
   strips
2 stalks celery, cut into 1-inch
   pieces
1 green pepper, cut into 1-inch
   strips
1 can (3 3/4-ounces) black olives
6 small white onions, peeled
1/4 pound fresh green beans,
   halved
3/4 cup water
3/4 cup wine vinegar
1/4 cup vegetable oil
1 teaspoon olive oil
2 tablespoons sugar
1 garlic clove, pressed
1 teaspoon dried oregano
dash salt
dash pepper

In a large pot, combine all the ingredients and bring to a boil. Simmer covered for about 5 minutes. Cool and refrigerate the mixture in a large jar for a day or two. Serves 8.

Caesar Salad
Insalata alla Cesare

Caesar Cardini
Tijuana, Mexico

Caesar Cardini created the original Caesar Salad on July 4, 1924 at Caesar's Palace in Tijuana, Mexico, which during Prohibition was a very popular place. Caesar Cardini's panache in the presentation of his original salad left his spectators in awe. Thus was born the Caesar salad.

The original salad was created when Mr. Cardini found that his supply of fresh vegetables wouldn't serve his big crowd. He gathered up some of the staples available in all good Italian kitchens and decided to give his dinner guests a show as well as a meal. The dramatic flourishes he used to combine the vegetables, oil, eggs, and croutons were so spectacular that the salad became a rage from coast to coast.

Film stars Jean Harlow, Clark Gable, and W.C. Fields came to visit this scene. Even Julia Child and her parents arrived to see the salad created in 1926.

When Caesar Cardini came to Los Angeles in 1939 to open a gourmet food store, people brought in empty bottles to be filled with the dressing.

Caesar Cardini and his daughter Rosa took the original Caesar Salad Dressing one step further when they created a bottled version of the dressing. Cardini's Original Caesar Salad Dressing is now available in gourmet food shops. The Cardinis also developed 10 other very tasty dressings.

This is the Caesar Salad Recipe from Caesar and Rosa Cardini:

2 medium-sized heads romaine lettuce (throw outer leaves away)
1/2 cup garlic-flavored oil
1/2 teaspoon freshly ground pepper
1/2 teaspoon salt
6 to 8 tablespoons freshly grated Parmesan cheese
2 coddled eggs (raw eggs boiled one minute)
8 to 10 drops Worcestershire sauce
juice of 2 medium-sized lemons
1/2 cup croutons

Break the romaine lettuce (cold, dry, and crisp) into 2-inch lengths or use the whole inner leaves. Then pour the garlic-flavored oil over the romaine. Sprinkle pepper and salt over the lettuce. Toss gently 2 to 3 times. Break the 2 coddled eggs into the lettuce and add the 8 to 10 drops Worcestershire sauce and the lemon juice, and toss 2 to 3 times. Sprinkle Parmesan cheese over the salad. Add the half cup of croutons, toss once again, arrange on chilled dinner plates, and serve immediately. Serves 4. Enjoy!

Garlic-Flavored Oil: Marinate 4 to 5 large cloves in 1 1/2 cups of good virgin olive oil. Cover and let stand for 4 to 5 days. Remove garlic.

Coddled Eggs: Bring a small pan of water to boil. Take the pan off heat and add two eggs in the shell. After 1 minute, remove the eggs from water and set aside.

Spaghetti Dinners
and a Wind-up Gramophone
by Marti Milani

My memories of Italian America are an endless feast—spaghetti dinners with homemade bread in the farmhouse of my grandfather's bachelor friend, Nick Titone; helping Aunt Nina make noodles or ravioli for Sunday dinner in Granddad's villa in Iowa; Easter morning pastries featuring whole hard-boiled eggs Nick had left on our porch; Nick's Christmas jars of mushrooms, pickled with garlic and peppers, and doled out carefully to last until spring; fragrant grapes from the enchanted corridor of Granddad's arbor; fresh squash blossoms dipped in batter and fried; and the delights of Granddad's ice cream parlor, created with chocolate of his own making and roasted nuts.

My grandfather, Santi Milani, expressed himself and his native country in that ice cream parlor in Centerville, Iowa. He came to America in the 1880s as a plaster of Paris artist for the World Expositions. In his ice cream parlor he added his own creations to the murals of Venice, the marble counters, and an elaborate tile floor. Italian opera arias from a wind-up gramophone completed the atmosphere of la dolce vita.

My grandmother died in my father's infancy, and "Aunt Nina," the housekeeper hired to care for the three motherless boys, came from Italy to America and stayed.

She presided over a house filled with heavy, hand-crocheted bedspreads and pillow shams, Venetian glass paperweights and stereopticon views of Rome. It was Aunt Nina who ordered the necessary ingredients from the Italian markets of large cities to create the wonderful food that evoked Italia in the American Midwest.

Tomato Sauce
Salsa di Pomidoro

Illinois Women's Chapter
National Italian American
Sports Hall of Fame
Arlington Heights, Illinois

2 tablespoons olive oil
1/2 cup finely chopped onions
2 cups Italian plum tomatoes
  or whole packed tomatoes,
  undrained, coarsely chopped
3 tablespoons tomato paste
1 tablespoon finely cut fresh basil
1 teaspoon sugar
1/2 teaspoon salt
freshly ground black pepper

In a 2- to 3-quart stainless steel saucepan, heat the olive oil until a light haze forms over it. Add the onions and cook them over moderate heat for 7 to 8 minutes or until they are soft but not browned. Add the tomatoes, tomato paste, basil, sugar, salt, and a few grindings of pepper. Reduce heat to very low; simmer for about 40 minutes with the pan partially covered. Stir occasionally. Press the sauce through a fine sieve or food mill into a bowl or pan. Season to taste and serve hot. Makes 3 cups.

Romolo, Remo, Trieste and Scranton

by Rom Russo

The poetry of Virgil records an ancient legend: the twins Romulus and Remus, born to a virgin, abandoned beside a river, and suckled by a she-wolf, grew to manhood and founded Rome.

From a very early age, I recall my father reciting the story of my birth. On August 8, 1915, shortly after midnight, twin boys were born to Augustino Nicolo Russo and Maria Parella Russo.

In the Italian community of Scranton, Pennsylvania, the anticipated birth was commonly known throughout. My father, a sculptor and a member of the Vittorio Alfieri Club, was rather highly regarded in the Italian community. As a result, the birth of the children was announced in the early morning hours in the Vittorio Alfieri Club, and from some unknown stimulus the words were uttered, "Trieste Trento."

Trieste and Trento were Italian cities under the domination of Austria. Italy was fighting in World War I to get those two cities back. With a hue and a cry, Trieste and Trento were to be the names of the two boys.

As I recall, my father told us in very dramatic fashion and with tears in his eyes how he felt duty bound, and announced that he would name the twin boys Trieste and Trento. Suddenly the gathering of Italians at the Vittorio Alfieri Club at that early hour erupted into a street parade. They marched through the streets of the Italian community singing *Trieste e Trento*, which was similar to the hue and cry that was being uttered throughout Italy at the time. I suspect that the Irish community and the Irish Police Force thought they had a revolt on their hands, when in truth and in fact, it was a joyous occasion.

Thereafter, in more quiet reflection, my father thought that to affix such names to his two children would be a little too spectacular and sensational and hard to comprehend by most Americans. So he changed the names to Romolo Nicholas Trieste Russo and Remo Trento Russo, and thus, the two twins bore those names which, of course, no one would think the least bit spectacular.

I've always been thankful I'm an Italian. We are the most exciting people on earth.

(Rom Russo, an attorney, practices in Dubuque and Iowa City, Iowa. His twin brother is deceased).

White Clam Sauce
Salsa Bianca con Vongole

Romolo Nicholas Trieste Russo

1 cup olive oil
8 to 10 cloves garlic
3 cans baby clams, drained
1 tablespoon chicken bouillon
finely chopped fresh parsley
coarsely ground pepper
red pepper
1 pound linguini

Brown the 8 to 10 cloves of garlic and the baby clams in the olive oil. Add the chicken bouillon and the parsley. Apply a fair measure of coarsely ground pepper and a very slight measure of red pepper and let simmer for 30 to 40 minutes. Cook the linguini in boiling salted water until *al dente*. Drain and place the cooked clam sauce thereon, and enjoy the nearest thing to heavenly precincts. Serves 4.

Note: If fresh clams are used, then carefully rinse 2 to 3 dozen clams to remove sand, place in a pan with a cup of water on the bottom, and steam until all the clams are opened. Remove the meat. Retain the juice and use as directed above.

Pesto Sauce
Pesto

*Carol Butera
Illinois Women's Chapter
National Italian American
Sports Hall of Fame
Arlington Heights, Illinois*

1/2 cup olive oil
3 cloves garlic
1/4 teaspoon salt
2 cups firmly packed fresh basil
   leaves
2 tablespoons pignoli (pine nuts)
   or walnuts
2/3 cup grated Parmesan cheese

Place the oil, garlic and salt in an electric blender or food processor and whirl until smooth. Add the basil and nuts. Blend until smooth. Transfer to a bowl; fold in the Parmesan cheese. Spoon the pesto over 1 pound of hot, cooked, drained pasta. Toss until evenly blended. Serve immediately with additional Parmesan cheese. Makes about 3 cups.

*Italian Market,
Boston, Massachusetts*
Photograph by Harry Oster.

Tomato and Onion Sauce
Filetti di Pomodoro

*Mario's Restaurant
Bronx, New York*

8 cups canned tomatoes,
   preferably imported from Italy
1/4 pound lard
3 cups thinly sliced onion
1/3 pound ham, preferably
   prosciutto, cut into very thin
   strips, about 1 1/2 cups
salt to taste
freshly ground pepper to taste
1/4 cup freshly snipped basil leaves
   or 1 tablespoon dried
   crushed basil

Using your hands, crush the tomatoes. Heat the lard and add the onions. Cook, stirring often, until the onions are golden brown, about 20 minutes. Add the ham and cook 5 minutes. Add the tomatoes and cook about 2 hours, stirring often to prevent sticking. Add the salt, pepper, and basil. Makes about 6 cups of sauce.

Bolognese Sauce
Salsa Bolognese

North Beach Restaurant
San Francisco, California

North Beach Restaurant is near Fisherman's Wharf. It is operated by Lorenzo Petroni and Chef Bruno Orsi. They serve "the best cucina Toscana possible." They cure their own prosciutto and prepare their own desserts. They have an extensive list of Italian and California wines.

1 small onion, chopped
1 small stalk celery, chopped
1 small carrot, chopped
cooking oil
1/2 pound ground veal
1/2 pound ground beef
1 cup chopped *pancetta*
2 cups or more chopped
    tomatoes, fresh or canned
pinch nutmeg
pepper
16 ounces pasta
white sauce or cream to taste
Parmesan cheese

Brown the chopped vegetables in oil, and add the veal, beef, and *pancetta*. Cook over low heat until cooked through. Add the tomatoes, nutmeg, and pepper. Simmer about 30 minutes, stirring occasionally. Cook the pasta as directed on the package. Rinse and drain. Add the sauce, white sauce or cream to taste, Parmesan cheese and toss to coat. Serve hot. Serves 4 to 5.

Meatballs a la DiPrete
Polpette alla DiPrete

The Honorable
Edward D. DiPrete
Governor of Rhode Island and
Providence Plantations
Providence, Rhode Island

Sauce:
2 tablespoons olive oil
1 clove garlic
1 large can stewed tomatoes
2 cans tomato paste
1 teaspoon sugar
2 bay leaves
pinch basil

Meatballs:
2 pounds hamburger
4 eggs
1 cup bread crumbs
1 stalk celery, chopped
1 onion, chopped
1 clove garlic, chopped
basil to taste

Sauce: Using a large pot, fry the whole garlic clove in oil. Remove and discard the garlic. Add the remaining ingredients and simmer on low heat 1 to 3 hours, stirring often. Add the cooked meatballs to the cooking sauce.
Meatballs: Mix the ingredients together. Shape into meatballs and fry or bake until brown. Add to the cooking sauce. Makes about 24 meatballs. Enjoy!

"La migliore parola e quella che no si dice."
"The best word is that which is not spoken."
—Congressman Frank Annunzio
Eleventh District
Chicago, Illinois

The Fireworks Family

When Angelo Lanzetta of Bari, Italy, a southern seaport, immigrated to America through Ellis Island in 1870, he would never have dreamed his descendants would be in charge of the fireworks for the bicentennial celebration of America's independence and the Statue of Liberty Centennial.

Angelo settled in Elmont, Long Island, New York, and sold fireworks. After Angelo's death, his son Anthony and Angelo's nephew Felix Grucci carried on the fireworks business. Felix, who also worked as a drummer in a local band, married Concetta DiDio and their three children, James, Donna, and Felix, Jr., all entered the family business at One Grucci Lane in Brookhaven, New York, on Long Island.

Felix invented the stringless shell, eliminating burning fallout, and developed for the United States Defense Department an atomic device simulator for troop training.

The Gruccis became the first American family to win the Gold Medal for the United States at the Monte Carlo International Fireworks Competition in 1979.

The Gruccis did the fireworks for the Lake Placid Winter Olympics, the World's Fair in Knoxville, Tennessee, the Los Angeles Summer Olympics, the inaugurations of Presidents Ronald Reagan and George Bush, and the Brooklyn Bridge Centennial. Harvard University had a Grucci lighting for the institution's 350th anniversary. Many American cities have Grucci Fireworks for Fourth of July celebrations. Grucci fireworks opened the boating season in Seattle.

According to the sponsoring Pepsi Cola National Convention planners, Grucci fireworks lit up the San Francisco Harbor "in a style that will long be remembered by the Bay City inhabitants."

Edward Koch, mayor of New York, wrote the Gruccis that "the fireworks display at the Brooklyn Bridge was absolutely spectacular. No one has seen anything like it. I am pleased to know that Commissioners Ameruso and Spinnato were helpful. My congratulations on what was literally a bang-up job."

Clara's Italian Meatballs
Polpette di Chiara

Clara Grucci
Brookhaven, New York

1 cup rolls
1 1/2 pounds chopped meat
1 egg
4 ounces Parmesan cheese, grated, more if preferred
1 teaspoon salt
1 dash pepper
2 cloves fresh garlic, minced
fresh Italian parsley
1 cup Italian seasoned bread crumbs
oil for frying

Run the rolls under warm water; squeeze out the excess water. Place the remaining ingredients in a mixing bowl and mix. Add the wet rolls and mix thoroughly. Roll into balls and fry in hot oil. These can be frozen. Serves 4.

Breads & Pizzas

The Befana Legend

In the costume and role of a Befana at the Italian Christmas pageant at the Museum of Science and Industry in Chicago, Rose Cuzzone of Elmhurst, Illinois, has a basket of candy and gifts for good children. With her are Angelica, left, and Heather Marsala of Bolingbrook, Illinois. Befana, who was busy cleaning, refused to assist the Wise Men, then repented and, failing to find them and the Christ child, wandered Italy with presents at Epiphany. Mothers warn children Befana will give them a piece of coal and a switching if they are bad.

Festive Italian Christmas Bread
Panettone

Stephanie Balistreri
Milwaukee, Wisconsin

2 cakes (3/4 ounces each)
   compressed yeast or
   2 packages dry yeast
1 cup hot water, divided
1/2 cup butter or oleo, softened
1 cup sugar
2 teaspoons salt
4 eggs
1 1/2 teaspoons anise extract
6 1/2 to 7 cups sifted all-purpose
   flour
1/4 cup butter, melted
powdered sugar-milk glaze, optional
2/3 cup chopped almonds
1/2 cup each chopped dates,
   candied cherries, candied
   orange peels

Soften the yeast in 1/4 cup hot water. Combine the butter, sugar, salt, and the remaining 3/4 cup hot water in a large bowl. Stir until the butter melts and the sugar dissolves. Cool to lukewarm. Beat in the eggs one at a time and add the anise extract. Stir in 6 1/2 cups flour. Add the yeast mixture and as much of the remaining flour as you need to make a soft dough. Turn out onto a lightly floured board and knead until the surface of the dough is soft and elastic, about 5 minutes. Return the dough to the bowl. Rub the dough lightly with the melted butter, cover and let rise in a warm place until doubled in bulk, about 1 1/2 hours. Punch down and shape the dough into 2 round loaves, or 4 small loaves. Place on greased baking sheets. Brush lightly with the butter. Let rise until doubled in bulk, about 1/2 hour. Cut a slash in the top of each loaf. Bake in the center of the oven at 350° for 30 to 35 minutes or until the bread tests done. Cool on a wire rack. Glaze the top of the bread with a powdered sugar-milk frosting. Decorate with whole almonds and candied fruit.

Crusty Italian Rolls
Panini

Rene Pagliai

2 packages yeast
1 cup lukewarm water, divided
1/2 cup scalded milk
1 1/2 tablespoons shortening or oil
2 tablespoons sugar
1 1/2 teaspoons salt
4 cups flour

Dissolve the yeast in 1/3 cup warm water and set aside until foamy. Beat together the remaining ingredients. Add the yeast. Mix until the dough forms a ball. Let rise until double in bulk. Divide the dough into 16 pieces and form into 4-inch rolls. Place on a baking sheet and let rise again. Bake at 350° for 20 minutes. Cool and freeze. Thaw and bake at 350° for 5 to 10 minutes or until warmed. The rolls become very crusty this way. Makes 16 rolls.

St. Joseph's Bread
Pane di San Giuseppe

Eunice McCarthy
Italian Women's Civic Club
Rochester, New York

10 cups flour, sifted
2 1/4 cups lukewarm water
2 packages dry yeast
2 teaspoons salt
1/4 cup anise seeds
1/4 cup salad oil
corn meal
1 egg yolk
1 tablespoon water

Sift the flour into a bowl. Stir the yeast into the water until it is dissolved. Make a well in the center of the flour and pour the yeast mixture, salt and anise seeds into the well. Mix with your hands until you have a dough, then knead for about 10 minutes until the dough is smooth and elastic. Pour the oil over the dough and knead until no longer sticky, about 5 minutes. Cover the dough with a clean towel and let it rise in a warm place until doubled in bulk. Divide the dough into 2 parts. Shape into 2 round loaves, or into the shape of a long beard, symbolic of the St. Joseph's beard. Sprinkle a little corn meal on the bottom of an ungreased baking pan and place the loaves on the corn meal. Brush the loaves before baking with a mixture of 1 beaten egg yolk and 1 tablespoon of water. Bake at 425° for 10 minutes, then reduce heat to 375° and bake until the loaves are golden brown and sound hollow when tapped, about 30 minutes. Cool on a rack.

Pizza in the Rustic Style
Pizza Rustica

Angela Giannone
Morton Grove, Illinois

"My husband Richard was a musician who loved music and held anyone associated with music in very high esteem. The one he admired most was Toscanini, conductor of the New York Philharmonic Orchestra. During and very shortly after the Second World War there was a serious shortage of good teachers. We decided to take our 7-year-old daughter Amelia out of public school and enter her in a parochial school. One day shortly thereafter she was at her cousin's house. Knowing that Amelia was now enrolled in a Catholic school, they asked her, 'Amelia, do you know who God is?' She promptly replied 'Toscanini.'
"My mother's Pizza Rustica was always made on holidays. I hope it meets with your approval. Good luck."

4 eggs, well beaten
1 1/2 cups grated Provolone cheese
1/3 cup Genoa salami, minced
1/3 cup capocollo, minced
1/3 cup prosciutto, minced
1/3 cup grated Parmigiano cheese
2/3 cup milk
pinch nutmeg
salt and pepper to taste
2 9-inch pie crusts, or 1 crust
    and strips for the top

Mix the first nine ingredients well. Place the mixture in the unbaked pastry shell. Place lattice strips on top. Bake at 400° for 15 minutes. Reduce the heat to 325° and bake 20 minutes more, or until golden brown. Cut in 1-inch cubes and serve as an hors d´oeuvre with a glass of wine. Serves 6 to 8.

Italian Sweet Bread
Panachia

Rene Pagliai

2 cups scalded milk
1/2 cup melted shortening
1 teaspoon salt
1/4 cup warm water
2 packages dry yeast
1/4 cup sugar
1/4 cup honey
2 eggs
1/2 cup candied fruit
1 cup white raisins
7 to 7 1/2 cups flour

Add the shortening and salt to the milk. Cool to lukewarm. Soften the yeast in 1/4 cup warm water, then add sugar. Add the yeast mixture to the milk mixture. Add the remaining ingredients and beat until the dough leaves the sides of the bowl. Let rise, covered, in a warm place until double in bulk. Divide into 2 loaves, let rise again until doubled in bulk. Bake at 375° for 35 minutes.

"Meglio tardi che mai."
Better late than never."
—Leonard Giampietro
Chicago, Illinois

Carmello Zingara serves pizza at the Milwaukee Holiday Folk Fair.

Broccoli-Ricotta Pizza Strudel

Pizza con Broccoli e Ricotta
Ralph Davino
Pompei Bakery
Chicago, Illinois

pizza dough, at right
1 1/2 cups prepared pizza sauce
    with basil
2 cups shredded mozzarella,
    divided
1 1/2 cups fresh broccoli, blanched,
    refreshed, cooled, and chopped
2 cups drained ricotta cheese
1 teaspoon salt
1 teaspoon pepper
1 cup grated Romano cheese
1/4 cup olive oil
1 egg

Punch the dough down. Roll it out on a lightly floured surface into a 12x17-inch rectangle. Place the dough rectangle in a lightly oiled baking pan. With a kitchen scissors, cut 3-inch slashes toward the center of the dough at 3-inch intervals down both long sides of the crust. Spread the pizza sauce over the solid center portion of the crust to point where slashes start. Spread 1 cup mozzarella over the sauce. Distribute the broccoli, ricotta, salt, pepper and Romano over the mozzarella. Top with the remaining mozzarella. Drizzle the olive oil over the filling ingredients.

To braid top crust: Starting at one end, fold a dough strip straight across to the opposite side. Cover that strip with the strip directly opposite it. Fold the remaining strips, pulling slightly at a slant, alternating sides. Fold the last two dough strips as the first two, straight across. Beat the egg in a small dish. Brush the top of the strudel with the beaten egg. Bake in a preheated 400° oven for 18 to 20 minutes until golden. Serve hot or at room temperature to 12 as an appetizer; 8 as a main course.

Pizza Dough

Pasta per la Pizza

1 envelope dry yeast
1 cup warm water
3 cups all-purpose flour plus
    additional flour for kneading
    if necessary
1 teaspoon salt
1 tablespoon olive oil

Mix the yeast with the warm water. Set aside until foamy. Place the 3 cups flour and the salt in a large mixing bowl. Make a well in the center. Pour the yeast mixture and olive oil into the well and mix to form a dough ball. Turn the dough out on a lightly floured surface. Knead for 10 minutes until smooth and elastic, working in additional flour if needed. Place the dough in a large oiled bowl. Cover and set aside to rise in a warm spot for 45 minutes until doubled in size.

Easter Pie
Calzone

Anna Gardaphe

Crust:
6 cups flour
3/4 cup sugar
3 1/2 teaspoons baking powder
1/2 teaspoon salt
4 eggs, slightly beaten
1 cup melted lard
1/2 cup lukewarm water or more
   if needed

Filling:
2 pounds ricotta cheese
1/2 teaspoon salt
dash black pepper
1/2 cup sugar
3 eggs
parsley, chopped, to taste
1 1/2 pounds sausage, sliced
1 dozen hard-cooked eggs, sliced

Topping:
2 egg yolks
sugar to taste

Crust: Sift together the dry ingredients and make a well. Pour the eggs, lard and water into the well. Knead together until well mixed. Cover and let stand while making filling.
Filling: Mix together all the ingredients except the sausage and eggs.
Assembly: Roll out the crust dough as one would to make a double pie crust. Make the bottom layer thicker than the top layer. Layer the ricotta mixture, then the sausage and sliced eggs. Roll out top crust and cover the pie. Seal the edges by pinching or pressing with the tines of a fork. Trim the excess crust.

Topping: Combine the topping ingredients and brush the pie. Bake at 350° for 1 1/2 hours. Makes 2 small pies.

Carmela's Homemade Bread
Pane di Carmela Fatto in Casa

Maria Carmela Bartucci
Norridge, Illinois

1 envelope dry yeast
about 1 quart warm water,
   divided
large pinch of salt, to taste
2 pounds unbleached flour

In a large bowl dissolve the yeast in about 1 cup water. Add the salt and flour. Next slowly add the water, mixing well until you have a smooth consistency. Knead well. Cover and keep in a warm place to rise, about 1 to 2 hours. Punch down, knead and form into loaves. Place the loaves on a cookie sheet sprinkled with flour and cover. Let the loaves rise for 20 minutes. Preheat the oven to 350°. After the second rise, slit the tops of the loaves and bake on the middle rack for 1 hour. Check the color of the loaves after 20 minutes; if they are baking too quickly, adjust the rack.
Variations: (1) Instead of forming loaves, form little cookie-shapes and deep fry. Drain on paper towels. Sprinkle with powdered or regular sugar.
(2) Form into mini-pizzas and place an anchovy fillet in the center. Fold over, press along the edges to close and fry.

Main Dishes

Veal Rosetto
Vitella Rosetto

*Frank DiSantis, owner-chef,
Cent'Anni,
Philadelphia, Pennsylvania, and
Norristown, Pennsylvania*

*"I was brought up in a restaurant
family of Italian descent and was
inspired by my family to express the
true tradition of my ancestors
through original recipes from their
homeland. This recipe is a dish for
special occasions originally created
by my grandmother."*

1/2 cup fresh mushrooms
1 whole tomato, skin removed
   by blanching
1 slice prosciutto
1/4 teaspoon white pepper
pinch fresh basil
2 ounces white wine, preferably
   Soave
3 1-ounce pieces of veal,
   pounded, lightly floured
3 medium-sized fresh shrimp
4 ounces Alfredo sauce, prepared
4 ounces tomato sauce, prepared
1 tablespoon sugar
4 ounces angel hair pasta,
   cooked
slice of orange
piece of kale
fresh chopped parsley

Combine the mushrooms, whole tomato, prosciutto, white pepper, and
basil. Mince to a fine mixture. In a
medium-sized saucepan add the
minced mixture and 2 ounces of
wine, veal medallions, and shrimp.
Sauté until the veal and shrimp are
fully cooked and the alcohol is
burned off. In a second, larger
saucepan combine the Alfredo
sauce, tomato sauce and sugar.
Stir to a consistent rose color, then
add the contents of the first pan.
Heat together for 45 seconds, stirring frequently, until the sauce starts
to bubble. Remove from the stove.
On a large oval plate place the
cooked angel hair pasta. From the
saucepan, remove the veal and
shrimp. Lay the veal in one row and
the shrimp in another atop the pasta.
Pour the contents of the pan over
the veal, shrimp and pasta. Garnish
with a slice of orange and a piece of
kale. Sprinkle with a pinch of fresh
chopped parsley. Serves 2.

According to Horace
(65-8 B.C.)

Use only eggs that are oval. They
have a better texture and a better
flavor.

Nothing is more tasteless than
stuff grown in a garden that has
been overwatered.

Plunge a tough fowl into a
Falernian wine mixed with water.
This will make it tender.

You can cure a hangover with
fried shrimps and African snails.

Veal Cutlets Sorrentino
Cotolette di Vitella alla Sorrentino

Ann Sorrentino

"This is my version of a dish served in a Neapolitan restaurant I visited in Italy in the 1970s."

8 veal cutlets
1 medium-sized eggplant
salt and pepper
3 4 cup flour
2 eggs, divided
1 tablespoon water
3/4 cup fine dry bread crumbs
5 tablespoons grated Romano
  cheese, divided
5 teaspoons chopped fresh
  parsley or 1 1/2 teaspoons
  dried parsley, divided
1 small clove garlic, finely minced
1 cup ricotta cheese, drained
1/2 cup olive oil, divided
1/2 cup salad oil, divided
4 slices mozzarella cheese

Marinara Sauce:
1/4 cup olive oil
1 clove garlic, minced
1 small can tomatoes, 2 cups
  or less, puréed
3/4 teaspoon salt
1/2 teaspoon oregano
1/4 teaspoon basil
1 teaspoon chopped parsley
fresh ground black pepper

Have your butcher prepare the cutlets about 1/4 inch thick and about 4 ounces each. Peel the eggplant and cut into lengthwise 1/4-inch slices. Sprinkle with salt. Season the veal with flour to which 1/2 teaspoon salt and 1/4 teaspoon pepper have been added. Flour the cutlets, shaking off excess flour. Set aside. Beat 1 egg with 1 table-spoon water. Set aside. Season the bread crumbs with 3 table-spoons grated Romano cheese, 3 teaspoons fresh or 1 teaspoon dried parsley, garlic, salt and pepper to taste and mix well. Dip the cutlets in the egg wash, drain excess and dip into the seasoned bread crumbs. Press the crumbs firmly into the cutlets and place on waxed paper to dry, about 30 minutes, turning once. Whip the ricotta with the remaining grated Romano, parsley, salt, and pepper to taste, and remaining egg. Set in the refrigerator until needed. Heat 1/4 cup each of the oils in a broad non-stick frying pan. When hot, cook the cutlets until they are golden brown color. Set aside. Add the remaining oil and heat until hot. Dip the eggplant slices in the remaining flour, shake off the excess and fry in the hot oil until golden. Place on paper towels.

Marinara Sauce: Heat the oil in a saucepan and gently cook the minced garlic until it starts to brown. Watch closely; do not burn. Add the tomatoes and seasonings. Cook rapidly uncovered until the liquid is condensed and the sauce is thickened. Stir occasionally to keep from sticking. Makes 1 cup.

Assembly: Place the cutlets in a baking dish or pan that will hold them without crowding. On each cutlet place 2 tablespoons of the ricotta mixture and cover with a slice of eggplant. Spoon sauce on each eggplant slice. Cut the mozzarella cheese slices in half. Place 1 piece on each cutlet. Bake in a 350° oven until the cutlets are heated through and the cheese is melted. Serves 8.

Veal Margherita alla Felicia

Vitello Margherita alla Felicia

*Felicia Solimines
Felicia's Restaurant
Boston, Massachusetts*

7 slices veal (about 1 1/2 pounds)
salt and freshly ground pepper
1/4 pound butter or more as
　needed
1/2 pound mushrooms, sliced
1 clove garlic
1/2 tablespoon fresh sage leaves
　or 1 teaspoon ground
　dried sage
14 very thin slices of lemon
1/4 cup dry white wine or brandy
rice or broccoli

Have your butcher pound seven veal slices as thin as possible, about 1/4 inch thick. Season them with salt and freshly ground pepper. Sauté the veal slices a few at a time in butter over a fairly high heat and cook until golden brown, about 2 minutes per side. Transfer the veal slices to the center of a hot serving platter and keep warm. Add to the frying pan the mushrooms, garlic, sage, and lemon slices. Add additional butter if necessary and sauté over moderate heat about 5 minutes. Add the wine or brandy, as desired. Sauté to reduce it slightly over high heat and pour over the slices of veal. Surround with rice or broccoli as desired. Serves 4.

Veal Florentine Style

Vitello alla Fiorentina

*Marcella Treanor
Urbandale, Iowa*

Marcella was born in Naples, Italy. She opened her restaurant, Marcella's, 6 years ago in Des Moines, Iowa. She features only Italian food as found in her family's homes in Italy. This dish was her uncle Armando Vitiello's favorite dinner.

6　4-ounce slices veal
6 thin slices prosciutto
6 slices mozzarella cheese
6 medium-sized tomatoes, cut into
　bite-sized pieces
1/2 cup olive oil
1/2 teaspoon salt
chopped fresh basil or 1 tablespoon
　dried basil

In a baking dish place the veal flat. On each piece add a slice of prosciutto and mozzarella. Cook the tomatoes, salt, and basil in oil; simmer 5 minutes. Pour over the veal and cover the baking dish with foil. Bake at 350° for 1 1/2 hours. Serves 6.

Note: This can be prepared ahead of time and kept in the refrigerator for use the same day.

*Street scene
New York City, New York*
Photograph by Renato Rotolo.

127

Baked Long Island Bluefish
Filetti di Pesci al Forno

*The Honorable Mario Cuomo
Governor of New York
Albany, New York*

This is a recipe used at the Executive Mansion.

Crumb Mixture:
1 pound plain bread crumbs
3 tablespoons paprika
1 teaspoon ground white pepper
1 teaspoon onion powder
1 teaspoon garlic powder
1 teaspoon ground thyme
1/2 teaspoon salt
1/2 cup sherry
1/2 cup melted butter

8 bluefish fillets
water
melted butter to drizzle

Crumb Mixture: Place all the dry ingredients in a bowl and mix with an electric mixer at the lowest speed. Add the sherry and melted butter. Mix until thoroughly absorbed. Place the bluefish, skin side down, on a sizzle platter. Add enough water to cover bottom of sizzle platter. Pack the crumb mixture on top of the bluefish fillets. Drizzle with melted butter. Place the fish in a preheated 350° oven. Bake for 25 minutes. Serve immediately. Serves 8.
Note: The crumb mixture will keep for weeks in the refrigerator and can be used on all seafood.

Sicilian bread baked in an outdoor oven in a Chicago suburb.

Pork Chops alla Mafalda
Costolette di Maiale alla Mafalda

*Mafalda Polloni is chef emeritus of the Seaward Inn,
Rockport, Massachusetts*

6 pork chops
4 tablespoons flour
1 cup milk
1 cup Italian seasoned crumbs
(the seasoning should contain salt, pepper, thyme, sage and oregano)
16-ounce can Italian stewed tomatoes
1 onion, chopped
2 cloves garlic, chopped
4 stalks celery, chopped
salt and pepper
1 teaspoon sugar

Trim the pork chops of fat, dip each into the flour, then the milk and finally the seasoned bread crumbs. Set aside. In a large Dutch oven or casserole, combine the stewed tomatoes, onion, garlic, celery, salt, pepper, and sugar. Place the pork chops on top of this mixture. Cover with foil. Bake at 300° for 1 1/2 to 2 hours. Remove the foil for the last 10 minutes of baking and brown by turning on the broiling unit for about 5 minutes. Do not overbrown. Check midway during baking. If the chops are drying out, add 1/2 cup water to the tomato mixture. Serves 6.

Steak Pizzaiola
Bistecca alla Pizzaiola

Sal Anthony's Restaurant
New York City, New York

Anthony benefits from an Italian-American extended family with ties to many Italian regions: a Sicilian grandmother, a Neapolitan aunt, a Milanese uncle and a Genoese great-aunt. Anthony says of this dish:
"This method has humble origins; I can remember my grandmother tenderizing tough inexpensive cuts of meat with the long simmering in a pizzaiola tomato sauce."
Steak Pizzaiola is a classic example of the peasant teaching the prince how to eat.

4 tablespoons olive oil
2 small steaks about 1 inch thick
4 cloves garlic, peeled and cracked
1/2 cup thinly sliced onions
1 tablespoon tomato paste
1 cup sliced fresh mushrooms
2 bell peppers, sliced lengthwise into 1/4-inch strips, steamed for 1 minute
1 1/2 cups peeled, roughly chopped tomatoes
1/2 cup water
2 tablespoons chopped Italian parsley
salt, pepper and oregano to taste

Heat the olive oil in a skillet. Brown the steaks over high heat, 1 1/2 minutes on each side. Remove the steaks from the skillet and set aside on a warm platter. Reduce the heat and add the garlic, cooking until lightly golden. Remove the garlic and set aside. Add the onions and cook until translucent. Add the tomato paste, cooking and stirring with a wooden spoon until the paste blends with the oil. Add the mushrooms and sauté for 1 minute. Add the peppers and sauté for another minute. Add the cooked garlic, chopped tomatoes, water, parsley, salt, pepper, and oregano. Bring to a simmer and let cook for 5 minutes. Add the steaks to the skillet and partially cover with a lid. Cook over medium heat, turning the steaks once, for about 5 minutes, depending on the degree of doneness desired. Serve the steaks topped with the sauce, mushrooms and peppers. Serves 2.

Italian Steak
Bistecca Italiana

Josephine Scalissi Grunewald

1 round steak, pounded thinly
1/2 cup bread crumbs
1/4 cup grated Romano cheese
1/2 teaspoon basil
1 teaspoon garlic powder
1/4 teaspoon oregano
salt and pepper to taste
2 eggs
the juice of 1/2 lemon
1/2 cup olive oil

Mix the dry ingredients in a medium-sized shallow bowl. Beat the eggs with lemon juice in another medium-sized shallow bowl. In a large skillet pour just enough oil to cover the bottom. Dip the steak in the egg then in the bread crumb mixture. Sauté over medium to medium-high heat. Brown on both sides. Serve with pasta and spaghetti sauce. Do not overcook. Serves 4.

Leg of Lamb Abruzzese
Cosciotto d'Agnello all'Abruzzese

Anthony Carsello
Chicago, Illinois

1/4 pound lean salt pork, diced
   and parboiled for 10 minutes
6-pound leg of lamb, boned and
   tied to hold its shape
3 cloves garlic, halved
6 sprigs rosemary
6 tablespoons oil
1 cup dry white wine
1 1/2 pounds tomatoes, peeled,
   seeded, drained and chopped
2 tablespoons chopped parsley
1 tablespoon fresh oregano or
   1 teaspoon dried oregano
salt and freshly ground pepper

Put the diced salt pork in a frying pan over medium heat. Shake the pan until the pieces are golden on all sides. Remove them with a slotted spoon and drain on absorbent paper. Make small slits in the lamb with a sharp knife and insert half-cloves of garlic and small sprigs of rosemary into each slit. Rub the lamb with a generous amount of salt. Heat the oil in a large pot over fairly high heat and brown the lamb on all sides. Add the wine and cook until almost evaporated. Add the tomatoes, salt pork, parsley, oregano, and enough water to come about 1/3 up the sides of the lamb. Season with salt and pepper, bring to a boil, cover the pot and reduce the heat to low and simmer for about 2 hours, or until the lamb is tender. Transfer the lamb to a hot platter, reduce the sauce over high heat for about 5 minutes, season to taste, and pour over the lamb.
Serves 6 to 8.

Chicken Cacciatore
Hunter's Style Chicken
Pollo alla Cacciatore

Mary Pucci Couchman, M.D.

1 4 to 5-pound fryer chicken
6 tablespoons olive oil
4 tablespoons flour
1/2 teaspoon salt
1/4 teaspoon pepper
1/4 teaspoon thyme
1 teaspoon rosemary
1/2 pound mushrooms
1 onion, chopped
1/2 cup dry white wine
1 12-ounce can Italian pear
   tomatoes
3 tablespoons brandy
3 sprigs Italian parsley, minced
2 cloves garlic, mashed
2 tablespoons butter

Cut up the chicken or use a pre-cut chicken. Heat the olive oil in a large frying pan. Combine the flour, salt, pepper, and thyme. Dust the chicken with the flour mixture. Fry the chicken in the olive oil with the rosemary. When golden brown remove from pan and set aside. Add the mushrooms and onion; cook until tender and slightly browned. Add the wine and tomatoes. Cook 5 minutes. Put the chicken back into the pan and heat through again. Add the brandy, parsley and garlic. Cover and cook slowly until the chicken is tender. Add the butter. This is delicious served on rice. Serves 6.
Note: This can be made ahead and reheated. The flavor improves on standing. Broccoli and tossed salad are a nice accompaniment.

Zuppa di Pesce
"A Fisherman's Feast"

Chef Larry Poli, Jr.
Poli's Restaurant
Pittsburgh, Pennsylvania

1 medium-sized onion, diced
3 medium-sized leeks, white
    part only, minced
2 teaspoons minced garlic
1/2 cup extra virgin olive oil
1/2 cup chablis
1 gallon fish stock
3 cups whole cored tomatoes,
    crushed
2 teaspoons chicken base
1 bay leaf
1 teaspoon saffron
dash Tabasco
2 teaspoons Dijon mustard
dash Worcestershire sauce
4 live 1 1/4 pound Maine lobsters
    in shell
1/2 pound uncooked lobster meat
1 pound littleneck clams
1 pound mussels
1/2 pound bay scallops
1 pound salmon fillets, cut into
    2 ounce pieces
1 pound halibut fillets, cut into
    2 ounce pieces
salt and pepper to taste

Sauté the onion, leeks, and garlic in oil. Add the white wine and reduce the heat by half. Add the fish stock, tomatoes, chicken base, bay leaf, saffron, Tabasco, mustard, and Worcestershire. Stir well. Add in layers in this order: the live lobsters, the lobster meat, clams, mussels, scallops, salmon, and finally the halibut on top. Cover and bring to a boil. Remove the lid, and reduce the heat to a simmer. Simmer for 25 minutes. Add salt and pepper to taste. Serves 8.

Baked Florida Pompano with Fennel and Prosciutto
Pesce di Florida Al Forno
con Finocchio e Prosciutto

Chef Larry Poli, Jr.

Many years have passed since 1921, when Joseph Poli, from Lucca, Italy, established a luncheonette in Pittsburgh, Pennsylvania. In 1925 he married Mary Tambellini Poli and they have been partners in the business ever since. Poli's is now under the management of their grandsons.

2 whole pompano, 1 pound each,
    cleaned, heads removed
3 tablespoons extra virgin olive oil
2 cloves garlic, minced
1/2 cup fennel leaves, minced
1 cup fresh, soft bread crumbs
3 slices prosciutto, slivered
1/2 teaspoon salt
1/4 teaspoon fresh ground pepper

Rinse the fish thoroughly. Preheat the oven to 450°. Heat the oil in a frying pan. Add the garlic and fennel and cook 1 minute. Add the bread crumbs and prosciutto. Toss to coat with oil. Add the salt and pepper and mix well. Let cool. Cut 2 "X" scores in one side of the fish and stuff with the mixture. Sprinkle rest of the mixture over fish. Bake for 35 minutes at 450°. Serve immediately. Serves 2.

Baked Zucchini
Italian Style
Zucchini al Forno all' Italiano

Ann Sorrentino

Ann Sorrentino, who writes a food column for Fra Noi, *the Chicago area Italian-American newspaper, is an expert on the cuisine of all the regions of Italy. She was born in the United States to Italian immigrant parents.*

4 or 5 narrow zucchini, 8 to 9
   inches long
salt
1 cup flour
1/2 cup plus 1 tablespoon olive oil
   or salad oil, divided
1 pound ground beef
1 small onion, minced
1 small clove garlic, minced
1 tablespoon parsley, chopped
pinch oregano
1/2 teaspoon dried basil or
   2 large fresh leaves, chopped
2 tablespoons Parmesan or
   Romano cheese
salt and pepper to taste

Quick Tomato Sauce:
1 1/2 to 2 pounds tomatoes
   or 1 large can tomatoes
1/3 cup olive oil
1 medium-sized onion, chopped
1 large clove garlic, minced
4 or 5 large mushrooms,
   sliced, optional
1/4 cup plus 2 tablespoons grated
   Parmesan cheese, divided
3 large basil leaves, chopped
3 large mint leaves, chopped
1/4 teaspoon oregano
1 tablespoon chopped
   fresh parsley
1 teaspoon sugar
salt and pepper to taste

Select firm fresh zucchini no more than 1 1/2 to 2 inches in diameter. Large zucchini are too seedy for this recipe. Lightly scrape the skin and wash. Remove the ends, then cut into diagonal slices about 1/4 inch thick. Sprinkle the slices lightly with salt, then shake a few slices at a time in a bag containing flour. Pour 1/2 cup oil into a broad frying pan and heat over medium-high heat. When the oil is sufficiently hot add the zucchini slices, being sure to shake off any excess flour. Brown on both sides and continue until all the slices are cooked. Set aside. Prepare the meat by heating the 1 tablespoon of oil, then adding the onion and garlic. Sauté for 2 to 3 minutes over medium heat. Add the meat and all the seasonings, except the cheese. Continue to cook, stirring occasionally until it begins to brown. Add the cheese and stir to combine with the meat. Set aside. Drain off any accumulated fat from the meat.

Quick Tomato Sauce: Plunge the washed tomatoes into boiling water for no more than 1 minute. Run cold water over them and then remove the skins. Cut the tomatoes in half and squeeze the seeds and juice into a pot. Dice the tomato pulp and add a little more than half of it to the juice. Set the rest of the tomato aside until later. Cook the tomato juice over medium heat, stirring occasionally, until it is reduced to half. Heat the oil, add the onion and the garlic, and cook a minute or two. Add the mushrooms if desired and cook another 2 minutes. Add the tomato sauce and the balance of the diced tomatoes and bring to a boil. Add all the remaining ingredients and cook over medium heat until the sauce is of a medium-thick consistency. Set aside.

To assemble the casserole: Use either an oblong or round oven-proof dish and start by putting a layer of the sauce on the bottom of the dish. Layer the zucchini slices close together, cover with grated cheese and a little chopped basil and mint leaves. Add the meat and cover with a little sauce. Make another layer of zucchini slices. Repeat with sauce, cheese and chopped herbs. Bake at 350° for 20 minutes or until bubbly hot. Allow to stand a few minutes, then serve. Serves 6.

Note: This casserole may be prepared a day in advance and refrigerated. Remove from the refrigerator and bring to room temperature before baking. Any leftover sauce may be used with other vegetables, such as cooked string beans. This sauce can be used as a quick spaghetti sauce.

Eggplant Parmigiana
Melanzane alla Parmigiana

Lena Ales
Italian-American Society of
Jefferson Auxiliary
New Orleans, Louisiana

3 small to medium-sized eggplants
2 1/2 cups seasoned Italian bread
 crumbs
sweet basil to taste
salt and pepper to taste
Parmesan cheese to taste
4 whole eggs
2 tablespoons milk
oil for frying
6 to 8 ounces mozzarella, sliced
2 cups Italian tomato sauce

Peel and slice the eggplant into medium-sized slices. Set aside to drain. Mix the crumbs with the basil, salt, pepper, and Parmesan cheese. Beat the eggs with the milk. Dip each slice of eggplant into the egg mixture, then into the bread crumbs. Bread both sides. Re-dip into the eggs and bread crumb mixture. Fry each slice in hot cooking oil. Lightly brown both sides. Place a layer of the cooked eggplant into deep baking dish, and cover with a layer of mozzarella cheese. Continue with a layer of each and top with the cheese. Pour the Italian tomato sauce over the entire dish. Cover and cook in a preheated oven at 350° for about 30 to 45 minutes. Serves 5.

Gilda DiCicco of Chicago holds a loaf of Italian bread—Treccia Pane.

Spaghetti with Shrimp and Mushrooms
Spaghetti con Gamberi e Funghi

The Elenian Club
New Orleans, Louisiana

1 tablespoon salt
3 quarts boiling water
8 ounces spaghetti
1/2 cup butter or margarine
2 cloves garlic
6 large mushrooms, diced, or 1 can (6-ounces) mushrooms, drained
1 pound raw shrimp, shelled, cleaned and diced
1 teaspoon salt
1 teaspoon pepper
1/4 cup grated Parmesan cheese
parsley, chopped, optional

Add the tablespoon of salt to the rapidly boiling water. Gradually add the spaghetti so that the water continues to boil. Cook uncovered until tender. Meanwhile, melt the butter in a large skillet. Add the garlic, mushrooms, and shrimp. Cook over low heat 5 minutes or until the shrimp are pink. Sprinkle the seasonings over the mixture. Add the spaghetti and cheese using large fork to gently toss. Cook until heated through. If desired sprinkle with parsley. Serves 2.

Stuffed Squid
Calamari Imbottiti

Rose Saviano
Illinois Women's Chapter
National Italian American
Sports Hall of Fame
Arlington Heights, Illinois

Sauce:
4 tablespoons oil
1 clove garlic, minced
1 (No. 2) can plum tomatoes

8 medium-sized squid
2 cloves garlic, minced
1 cup bread crumbs
1 tablespoon minced parsley
2 tablespoons grated Romano cheese
salt and pepper to taste
1 egg, beaten

Sauce: Brown the garlic in oil; mash the tomatoes with a fork or put through a blender. Add to the garlic and simmer for 1/2 hour.
Squid: Clean the squid thoroughly. Combine the remaining ingredients; fill the cavity of each squid with the stuffing. Sew the squid closed or fasten with toothpicks. Place in baking pan; cover with sauce. Bake at 400° for 35 minutes or until tender. Serves 8.

Pasta Dishes

Fettuccine Zingara
Gypsy Style

Marra's Restaurant
Philadelphia, Pennsylvania

In 1921 Salvatore Marra emigrated from Naples as a stowaway. He had only a dime in his pocket and he threw that into the water off Ellis Island so that he could say he started in America with nothing.

With a few years of work he discovered that the lava bricks used in his oven in Naples were responsible for the unique taste of his pizza. So he sent for bricks from Vesuvius and his pizzeria, located to the south of Philadelphia's Little Italy, became a success, attracting Mario Lanza (known as Fred Cocozza in those days), Frank Sinatra, and others.

Marra's daughter Bianca and her husband Mario D' Adamo operate the restaurant today.

Dough:
1 1/2 cups flour, unsifted
1 egg
1 egg white
1 tablespoon olive oil
1 teaspoon salt
2 tablespoons water

Sauce:
2 tablespoons olive oil
1 clove garlic, mashed
1/4 cup chopped red bell peppers
handful of spinach, chopped
3 mushrooms, sliced
1 tomato, cut into wedges
1/4 cup white wine
1/4 cup veal stock
1 tablespoon butter
1 tablespoon grated Romano
   cheese
6 Sicilian olives

Dough: Place the flour into a large bowl and make a well in the middle. Break the egg and the egg white into the well. Begin to knead the dough with your hands, using water to clear your hands of sticky dough. Add the oil and salt after the dough has congealed somewhat. Knead the dough until it no longer sticks to your hands. With a rolling pin, roll the dough into very thin sheets. Cut the dough with a guitar string or a knife. Use flour liberally to keep the dough from sticking to the pin or knife. Hang the noodles to dry while making the sauce.

Sauce: Sauté the garlic, peppers, spinach, mushrooms and tomato in the oil until the garlic is browned and the other vegetables are tender. Add the white wine and veal stock; stir and cook over medium heat until the sauce is pasty. In boiling salted water cook the noodles until done, drain, and place onto a serving platter. Add the butter to the sauce, melt, and pour over the noodles. Sprinkle with the Romano cheese and garnish with the Sicilian olives. Serves 2.

Left: Bill Traverso, center, and his father, Louis, right, and uncle, Enrico, hold Italian sausages from San Francisco at their market in Santa Rosa, California.

Large Tortellini
Tortalacchi

Rene Pagliai

Filling:
1 pint steamed fresh spinach
1 small carton fresh ricotta cheese
    or 8 ounces of cottage cheese
1 tablespoon Parmesan cheese
1/4 cup chopped fresh parsley
1/2 teaspoon nutmeg
1 cup fresh bread crumbs

Dough:
2 1/2 cups flour
2 eggs
1 egg yolk
1 tablespoon oil
1 teaspoon salt

Filling: Drain the spinach. Add the remaining filling ingredients, mix well and set aside.

Dough: Put the flour in a large bowl and make a well. Whip together the remaining ingredients and pour into well. Mix together until a ball is formed. Let rest 1/2 hour. Roll out by hand or put through a pasta machine. Roll the dough very thin. Cut into 2 1/2-inch strips. Place small mounds of filling one inch apart down one side of the dough strips. Fold half the dough over to make a long strand of dough with little filling bulges and cut into squares. Bring opposite corners together, pinching to seal, to form the shape of a triangular hat. Set aside until all the *tortalacchi* are made. Boil water and add the *tortalacchi* until just done. Drain. Toss with melted butter and serve with freshly grated Parmesan cheese or spaghetti sauce. To freeze, place *tortalacchi* on a cookie sheet and freeze, then store in plastic bags. Makes 2 to 3 dozen.

Baked Lasagne Bolognese Style

Della Foppiano
Foppiano Vineyards
Healdsburg, California

"Northern Italians don't use mozzarella cheese," says Della Foppiano. "They like something 'cheesier,' and that's why I like this recipe with the Parmesan. It's so much creamier."

2 tablespoons butter
1 carrot, shredded
1 clove garlic, mashed
1 large onion, finely chopped
2 pounds lean ground beef
4 tomatoes, peeled and coarsely
    chopped
1 can (8 ounces) tomato sauce
1 teaspoon salt
1 teaspoon basil
1/2 teaspoon sugar
1/2 teaspoon oregano
1/2 cup Foppiano wine (red)
12 ounces lasagne
boiling salted water

Cream Sauce:
4 tablespoons butter
1 teaspoon salt
6 tablespoons flour
dash each pepper and nutmeg
3 cups milk
1 1/2 cups shredded Parmesan
    cheese

Heat the 2 tablespoons butter in a large frying pan. Add the carrot, garlic, and onion, and cook until soft, but not browned. Add the crumbled ground beef. Cook, stirring frequently, until all the red color is gone. Stir in the tomatoes, tomato sauce, salt, basil, sugar, oregano, and wine. Bring to a boil. Reduce the heat, cover and simmer for 1 hour. Uncover and cook 30 minutes longer until the sauce is thick. Skim off the fat. Meanwhile, cook the lasagne in a large quantity of boiling salted water until just tender. Drain and rinse with cold water, then separate noodles.

Cream Sauce: In a 2-quart saucepan, melt the 4 tablespoons butter. Add the flour, salt, pepper, and nutmeg. Gradually add the milk, stirring constantly. Cook, stirring until thickened, then cook 2 minutes longer. Stir in half the cheese. Arrange about 1/3 of the lasagne in a buttered 13x9-inch dish. Spread with about 1/3 the meat sauce and then with a third of the cream sauce. Make 2 more layers, finishing with the cream sauce on the top. Sprinkle with the remaining cheese. Bake at 350° for about 30 minutes until the top is browned. Cut into squares. This is great with wine. Serves 8.

Four generations of Foppianos have crushed grapes at their vineyard beside the Russian River, near Healdsburg, California, along the old Redwood Highway. Louis J. and Della Foppiano are shown with their son, Louis M., left, and daughter, Susan Valera, right, with her sons, James and Joey. In the foreground holding a wine bottle is grandson Paul Foppiano. Giovanni "John" Foppiano left Genoa, Italy in 1864, arriving by ship in Panama, where he walked overland to the Pacific. He then came by ship to San Francisco in time to head northeast to join the Gold Rush in Sonora, California. He worked in mines and searched riverbeds for gold. This search brought him down the Russian River to Healdsburg where he started growing fruits and vegetables. The winery began in 1896. During Prohibition, the Foppianos sold grapes. Today their wines are available in most states and in western Europe.

Spinach Lasagne
Lasagne di Spinace

Sabina LoCurto
Rochester, New York

Salsa Bolognese:
2 tablespoons butter
2 tablepoons oil
1 medium-sized onion, chopped
1 clove garlic, mashed
1/2 cup chopped celery
1/2 cup diced carrots
2 tablespoons minced parsley
2 bay leaves
1/4 pound prosciutto, minced
1/2 cup red wine
2 large cans (32 ounces) whole
    tomatoes, peeled
1 pound chopped beef (top
    round), cooked and crumbled
salt and pepper
1 cup grated Parmesan cheese

Spinach Pasta:
1 package (10 ounces) spinach,
    fresh or frozen, washed with
    stems removed
4 eggs
2 tablespoons oil
salt
3 to 4 cups flour

Bechamèl Sauce:
4 tablespoons butter
6 tablespoons flour
3 1/2 cups milk, hot
Parmesan cheese to taste
salt and pepper to taste

Salsa Bolognese: Sauté the onion and garlic in the butter and oil. Add the carrots, celery, parsley, and bay leaves; cook until soft. Add the prosciutto, wine; cook down. Add the tomatoes. Add the meat, salt and pepper; cook for about 45 minutes. Set aside.

Spinach Pasta: Steam the spinach in water from its own drippings. Squeeze out, and mince. Place in a blender, add the eggs, oil and salt to taste. Place 4 cups flour in a large bowl, make a well in the flour and pour the spinach mixture in the well. Mix together with your fingers or a fork until a rough dough ball is formed. Knead the dough, adding flour as needed, until the dough is smooth. Using a pasta machine, process the dough into lasagne strips, or roll out to 1/8 inch thickness and cut into 12x2 1/2-inch strips. Cook the noodles, one at a time in boiling salted water with 1 tablespoon oil in water to prevent sticking. After cooking, cool each strip in cold water.

Bechamèl Sauce: Melt the butter carefully, and add the flour, stirring with a whisk or wooden spoon until smooth. Add the hot milk and stir until smooth and thick. Add the Parmesan, salt, and pepper.

Assembly: In a greased 10x14-inch pan place a small amount of the Salsa Bolognese. Place 1/3 of the lasagne noodles over the top. Spread with 1/2 the Bechamèl Sauce, 1/3 the Salsa Bolognese, and 1/3 the grated Parmesan, repeat. Layer the last 1/3 of the noodles on top, spread with the Salsa Bolgnese and sprinkle with the last of the Parmesan. Bake at 350° for 20 minutes or until the lasagne is golden. Allow it to sit for 10 minutes before serving. Serves 8.

Gino's Fried Spaghetti
Spaghetti Fritti alla Gino

Gino Bartucci
Chicago, Illinois

3 tablespoons extra-virgin olive oil
1 medium-sized onion,
    thinly sliced
2 teaspoons minced garlic
1/2 pound imported spaghetti,
    uncooked
1 (16-ounce) can plum tomatoes,
    chopped with juice
1/4 cup ripe olives, pitted and
    halved
3 tablespoons drained capers
1 1/2 cups water
hot red pepper flakes
salt and pepper
1/4 cup chopped fresh basil or
    parsley
grated Parmesan cheese

Select a skillet wide enough to hold
the spaghetti. Heat the oil in the
skillet. Sauté the onion and garlic
for 5 minutes until soft. Remove
with a slotted spoon and reserve.
Place the spaghetti in skillet. Sauté
for 5 minutes, shaking the pan constantly, until some of the spaghetti
strands are golden. Add the re-
served onion, garlic, tomatoes with
juice, olives, capers, and 1 1/2 cups
water. Season to taste with the hot
pepper flakes, salt and pepper.
Cover and simmer over medium
heat for 15 minutes, stirring occasionally with a wooden fork or spoon
until the spaghetti is tender but still
firm. When the spaghetti is almost
cooked, toss in the basil or parsley.
Garnish with the grated cheese.
Serves 4 to 6 as an appetizer or side
dish.

Fresh Basil Pasta
Pasta con Basilico Fresco

Sabina LoCurto

*My mother from Abruzzi, near
Rome, made this recipe every year
at basil and tomato time.*

2 cups packed fresh basil leaves,
    washed
6 cups flour
8 eggs
salt
2 tablespoons oil

Boil the basil leaves with a little
water about 10 minutes or until
cooked and almost dry. Squeeze
out any excess water and set aside.
Sift the flour onto a board and make
a well in the center. Drop in the
eggs, salt, oil and the basil. Mix well
with a fork to make a stiff dough.
Knead 15 minutes until smooth and
pliable. Roll into 2 to 3 balls, cover
and place on a floured board to rest
about 1 hour. Roll out and put
through a pasta machine to make a
dough about 1/16th inch in thickness. Then put the dough through
1/4-inch noodle cutter on machine.
Cook the noodles in boiling salted
water for about 2 to 4 minutes and
serve with fresh tomato sauce.
Note: The pasta can be frozen and
dropped directly into boiling water
without thawing. Add 1 tablespoon
of oil to prevent sticking.

Potato Dumplings
Gnocchi di Patate

Mario's Restaurant
Bronx, New York

The Migliuccis are a family of chefs. Mario and Clemente, brothers, and Joseph, son and nephew, are the principals at Mario's Restaurant in the East Fordham section of the Bronx. Mario's has one of the best Neapolitan-style kitchens. Eighty years ago Mario's grandparents opened the first Italian restaurant in Egypt. Two-year-old Mario worked in the kitchen.

3 large potatoes, preferably Idaho
salt to taste
2 egg yolks
1 3/4 to 2 cups flour
6 tablespoons melted butter,
     optional
grated Parmesan cheese, optional
2 cups filetti di pomodoro sauce;
     see recipe on page 117
freshly ground black pepper

Place the potatoes in a kettle and add cold water to cover. Add the salt to taste and bring to a boil. Simmer until the potatoes are tender but not mushy. Drain and let cool. Peel the potatoes. Put them through a ricer, food mill or a meat grinder, using the medium blade. Add the egg yolks and blend well. Scoop the flour onto a flat surface. Start kneading the potatoes, adding the flour gradually, only enough to make a firm, soft, and delicate dough. If too much flour is added the potatoes become tough when cooked. Knead thoroughly, then shape the dough, rolling with the palms to make a thick sausage shape about 11 to 12 inches long. Using a knife or pastry scraper cut the roll into 11 equal slices. Roll each slice into a long cigar shape. Cut each cigar shape into 18 or 19 pieces. These pieces will resemble miniature pillows. Flour the pieces and set aside until ready to cook. Drop the pieces of dough, half of them at a time, into a large quantity of boiling salted water and let cook until they rise to the surface. Drain quickly and chill under cold running water. Drain well. When ready to serve, drop the pieces once more into a large quantity of boiling salted water. When they float the second time, drain them and place them in a serving dish. Add the melted butter and cheese, if desired. Add the sauce and sprinkle with pepper. Serve with additional sauce on the side. Serves 6 or more.

Risotto
Rice

Rachel Ann Seghesio
Cloverdale, California

Chicken Broth:
1 stewing hen
3 quarts water
2 carrots
2 stalks celery with leaves
1 onion, quartered
1 leek

Rice:
2 cups dried mushrooms
1 large onion, minced
1/2 cup butter
3 cups rice
salt and pepper
1 1/2 cups grated Parmesan cheese

Chicken Broth: Place the stewing hen in a stock pot with the water. Simmer for 45 minutes. Add the carrots, celery, onion, and leek. Simmer for 1 1/2 hours. Strain the broth and skim off the fat.

Rice: Soak the mushrooms in hot water for 15 minutes and then thinly slice. Sauté the onion in the butter. When delicately brown add the mushrooms and cook about 15 minutes. Add the rice and stir constantly for about 15 minutes. Add the chicken broth 1 cup at a time, cook for about 45 minutes. Add the salt and pepper. When the rice reaches the *al dente* (chewy) stage, remove from the heat and add the Parmesan cheese. Serve immediately and pass more cheese. Serves 10 to 12.

Note: The chicken broth can be made the day before. If made the day before, refrigerate, and skim off the fat the next day.

A Century of Winemaking

In 1886 Eduardo Seghesio left the Piedmont region of Italy and came to Asti, California, to work at the Italian Swiss Colony there.

For three years Eduardo worked at the Italian Swiss Colony, and received his room and board, but no pay. At the end of the three years, he received a lump sum payment. He continued working at the Colony. In 1893 he married Angela Dionisia Vasconi, and in 1894 he used his "lump sum payment" and other savings to buy 56 acres at Chianti, California.

First they sold grapes, and soon they started the small winery that more than a century later is still selling wines. They built a Victorian

The Seghesio family home and vineyards, Chianti, California

home now occupied by their son Eugene Pete and his wife, Rachel Ann. Rachel Ann says:

"Angela Seghesio would often prepare *risotto* for wine buyers who traveled by train from San Francisco to Chianti in the early 1900s. She raised her own chickens and would use one in making *risotto*. Chickens, when old, have lots of flavor. Living in the original Seghesio family home—I am now known as 'Mama'—cooking and preparing dinner for many guests involved in the wine business all over the United States, I often serve *risotto*, and our guests enjoy it."

Seghesio descendants today raise grapes on 350 acres in six locations, all in Sonoma County. They produce many kinds of wines, and welcome visitors at a century-old winery in Healdsburg that is a virtual museum, with some of the oldest and some of the most modern winemaking equipment.

141

Stuffed Pasta Pockets
Ravioli

Estelle Jacklin
National Italian American
Sports Hall of Fame,
Arlington Heights, Illinois

Ravioli Filling:
1 1/2 cups ricotta cheese
3/4 cup freshly grated imported
　Parmesan or Romano cheese
3 egg yolks
1 1/2 teaspoons salt

Pasta:
1 1/2 cups unsifted all-purpose
　flour
1 egg
1 egg white
1 tablespoon olive oil
1 teaspoon salt
few drops water

Filling: Combine all the ingredients. Mix well and set aside.
Pasta: Pour the flour into a large bowl. Make a well in the center of the flour. Combine the egg, egg white, oil, and salt; pour into the well. Using your fingers or a fork mix together until the dough can be gathered into a rough ball. Moisten any remaining dry bits of flour with the drops of water and press into the ball. Knead the dough on a floured board; add flour if necessary. After about 10 minutes the dough should be smooth, shiny, and elastic. Wrap in waxed paper; let rest for at least 10 minutes before rolling out. Divide into 4 pieces; roll out the first quarter as thin as possible; cover with a damp cloth to prevent it from drying out. Roll the second quarter of dough to a similar size and shape. Using the first sheet of rolled-out pasta as a sort of checker board, place a mound of the cheese filling, about 1 teaspoon, every 2 inches across and down the pasta. Brush the dough with water between the cheese mounds, using enough water to wet the lines evenly. Carefully spread the second sheet of pasta on top of the first. Press down firmly along the wetted lines. With a ravioli cutter or knife, cut the pasta into squares along the wetted lines. Roll and fill the remaining quarters of dough as the first. To cook, drop the ravioli into 6 to 8 quarts of boiling salted water and stir gently with a wooden spoon to keep them from sticking . Boil for 8 minutes; drain. Serve with tomato sauce or butter and freshly grated cheese. Serves about 4.

Spaghetti with Roman-style Sauce
Spaghetti all'Amatriciana

1/4 cup chopped onion
1 small clove garlic, halved
2 tablespoons olive oil
1/2 cup chopped prosciutto
1 1/2 pounds Italian tomatoes,
　peeled and diced
salt and pepper to taste
1 pound spaghetti
1/2 cup grated Parmesan cheese
1/2 cup grated Romano cheese

Sauté the onion and garlic in the oil until golden, and remove the garlic. Add the prosciutto. Add the tomatoes, salt, and pepper. Simmer for 30 minutes, stirring occasionally. Cook the spaghetti in boiling salted water until just done. Toss the pasta with the sauce and cheeses. Serves 4.

Pasta Milanese

The Elenian Club
New Orleans, Louisiana

The Elenian Club was originally known as the "Circolo Elena di Savoia" in honor of Her Royal Imperial Highness, Queen Elena di Savoia of the Kingdom of Italy. After World War II this club became The Elenian Club of New Orleans. The club's objectives are to promote cultural, educational, civic, and social activities among its members.

Sauce:

3 medium-sized onions, chopped
3 tablespoons olive oil
2 cans (2 ounces each) anchovies
6-ounce can tomato paste
1 can (1 pound, 2 ounces) tomato
   purée
15-ounce can tomato sauce
2 1/2 cups water
1 teaspoon salt
1 teaspoon sugar
3/4 teaspoon pepper
4 to 5 fresh basil leaves or
   1/2 teaspoon dried basil
3 tablespoons currants, optional
1/2 tablespoon saffron, optional
1/4 cup pine nuts, optional
1 can macaroni seasoning
   with sardines*
1 small bunch fresh wild fennel
   (finocchio)
2 pounds perciatelli or bucatino
   pasta

Crumb Topping:

1 clove garlic, mashed
1 tablespoon olive oil
dash red pepper
seasoned bread crumbs
Parmesan cheese to taste

Sauce: In a heavy saucepan sauté the onion in the oil until translucent; add the anchovies. Fry slowly. Add the tomato paste, tomato purée, tomato sauce, water, salt, sugar, pepper, basil, and the optional ingredients. Simmer uncovered over moderate heat for 1 hour. Add the undrained can of macaroni seasoning with sardines. Cover and continue cooking over moderate heat another hour until sauce is thick. Makes approximately 8 servings or 2 quarts sauce.

In the meantime, wash and cut the fennel into small pieces. Cook in boiling salted water. When nearly tender, remove; add the perciatelli or bucatino and cook until just done. Drain in a colander; place in a serving bowl. Spoon the sauce over the pasta, sprinkle with the crumb topping, and enjoy.

Crumb Topping: Sauté the garlic in oil until browned; remove and discard. Mix the red pepper with the bread crumbs and add to the pan. Add the Parmesan cheese, cook until golden brown and serve over the sauce.
*Found in specialty food shops.

Olive branches.

143

Vegetable Dishes

Pickled Green Tomatoes
Pomidoro Verdi in Salamoia

Anna Stranieri
Iowa City, Iowa

water
green tomatoes
salt
fennel or anise seed
garlic
earthenware crock with non-metal
  lid to fit inside crock and a 2 to 3
  pound stone for weight.

Put 1/4 to 1/2 cup water in the crock. Add one layer of tomatoes cut cross-wise into slices 1/4 to 1/2-inch thick. Add one fistful of regular table salt; sprinkle over entire layer. Add about 1 teaspoon fennel or anise seed and at least 3 to 4 cloves of garlic, quartered. Add another layer of tomatoes and repeat the procedure until you have used all your tomatoes or the crock is filled. Place a piece of clean cotton cloth over the tomatoes, inside the rim of the crock, then put the lid on the cloth and the stone for weight. Set the crock in a baking pan to catch any overflow of the brine. As the tomatoes flatten due to the weight, you can add more and keep doing this till you have done as many as you want. It is important that the tomatoes always be submerged in the brine. It is nec-essary especially at the beginning to clean the stone, lid, and cloth, and to remove any scum that has formed. Every 2 to 4 days scum can be removed with a big spoon. When adding more liquid to the crock, always make up a solution of water

and salt. Do not add unsalted wa-ter. Keep in a cool dry place. Let set 6 to 8 weeks before using. A real treat is to eat as a snack with pep-peroni, Provolone cheese, Italian bread, and, of course, wine.

Escarole and Beans
Scarola e Fagioli

Donata Rotolo
Melrose Park, Illinois

1 to 2 heads escarole
16 ounces cooked beans, *fava*,
  navy or white
8 cloves garlic, mashed
1 cup olive oil
1 cup Parmesan cheese
6 eggs, slightly beaten

Clean and chop the escarole. Bring a pot of water to a boil and add the escarole. Strain 1/2 the water out and add the beans. In a saucepan, fry the garlic in the olive oil until browned. Add the contents of sauce-pan to the pot. Add the Parmesan cheese and eggs. Simmer until done, stirring occasionally. Serves 6.

Right: The staff of Fra Noi, the Ital-ian-American newspaper, is shown at Villa Scalabrini, Northlake, Illi-nois. The statuary honors "the mi-grant families who have touched the shores of this land."

Pickled Zucchini
Zucchini Sotto Aceto

Angela Giannone

"This is my mother's recipe. She was born and raised in a small town called Toritto Provincia di Bari. She came to America when she was about 20 years old. She always had mint in her garden so it was no trouble to add fresh mint to her zucchini."

2 pounds zucchini
3/8 cup oil
salt and pepper
1/2 cup wine vinegar
2 tablespoons sugar
1 clove garlic, cut in half
1 sprig mint or 1 drop mint extract

Wash the zucchini well, cut off the stems and slice in 3/8-inch slices. Fry in oil till delicately brown on both sides. Place in a deep serving dish with a cover and salt and pepper to taste. Set aside. In a saucepan boil the vinegar, sugar, and garlic for about 3 minutes, making sure the sugar is completely dissolved. Add the sprig of mint or extract, remove the garlic and pour over the zucchini. Chill and serve cold.

Stuffed Artichokes alla Siciliana
Carciofi Imbottiti alla Siciliana

Mary Spallitta
Chicago, Illinois

4 fresh artichokes
1 cup bread crumbs
1/2 cup grated Romano cheese
2 tablespoons chopped parsley
2 cloves garlic, chopped
olive oil
water or wine
salt and pepper to taste

Cut the stems from the artichokes and about 1 inch off the tips. Discard the tough outer leaves. Wash carefully and drain. Tap the artichokes on the table to spread leaves apart. Discard the fuzzy core. Mix the bread crumbs, cheese, parsley, garlic and 6 tablespoons of oil. Divide the stuffing equally among the artichokes. Fill center of the artichokes with stuffing. Place them upright in a saucepan to fit snugly. Pour 1 tablespoon of oil over each artichoke and add 1 cup of water or wine to the bottom of the pan. Cover tightly. Simmer slowly for about 30 minutes or until tender. Watch the water carefully, adding more if it evaporates. Season to taste. Serve hot. Serves 4.

Zucchini Squash Casserole
Zucchini in Casseruola

The Elenian Club
New Orleans, Louisiana

3 or 4 zucchini squash or 6 yellow
   squash
1 tablespoon butter
3 tablespoons flour
3 tomatoes, chopped
1/2 cup green pepper
1/2 cup onion
1 teaspoon salt
1/4 teaspoon pepper
1/2 teaspoon sugar
1/2 cup grated mozzarella
1/2 cup bread crumbs

Cook the unpeeled squash, drain
the water and slice; pat with paper
towel. Melt the butter and add flour,
vegetables, salt, pepper and sugar.
Cook until soft. Arrange the squash
slices in a square casserole dish
and pour the vegetables over the
squash. Sprinkle the cheese and
bread crumbs on top. Bake in a
350° oven until the cheese is melted
and the bread crumbs are golden.
Serves 8.

Stuffed Green Peppers
Peperoni Imbottiti

Josephine Scalissi Grunewald

*A school teacher raised in Madison,
Wisconsin, Jo had 11 brothers and
sisters born to parents who emigrated from Sicily in 1902.*

8 to 10 large green peppers
2 1/2 pounds ground beef
2 cups bread crumbs
2/3 cup grated Romano or
   Parmesan cheese
4 cups cooked white rice
1/2 cup onion, minced
1 teaspoon garlic powder or
   4 cloves garlic, crushed
2 teaspoons basil
1 teaspoon salt
1/2 teaspoon pepper
2 cups water
2 cups spaghetti sauce

Cut off the tops of the peppers and
clean out the seeds. Steam the
peppers until just done. Cool. Mix
the remaining ingredients, except
for the spaghetti sauce. Pour the
spaghetti sauce in a large pan. Being
careful not to split the peppers, stuff
and lower them gently into sauce.
Simmer, covered, for about 2 hours.
Stir carefully and occasionally during cooking time. Cut the peppers
in half, lay open on plates, and drizzle
with the spaghetti sauce. Pass additional grated cheese, if desired.

*In Gravesend, Brooklyn, New York,
this 1944 yard shrine was built in
thanks for the safe return of sons
serving in World War II. The present owners, Anthony and Clem-
intine Vespoli, maintain the shrine.*
Photograph © Joseph Sciorra 1987.

Desserts, Cakes & Cookies

Cannoli alla Siciliana

Felicia Solimines
Felicia's Restaurant
Boston, Massachusetts

Felicia feeds the famous. Twenty-five years ago Bob Hope became so enamored of her cooking that she has been invited to cook for Hope and his friends, including former President Gerald Ford, Efrem Zimbalist, Jr. and others. Frank Sinatra and Luciano Pavarotti are also good customers.

The word cannoli *means pipes. These pastries take the name from the round metal tubes or pipes around which they are rolled before being deep fried.*

Dough:
1 1/2 cups sifted all-purpose flour
pinch salt
5 tablespoons Marsala wine
1 tablespoon superfine sugar
oil for frying
12 *cannoli* pipes

Filling:
2 cups ricotta cheese, as fresh
    as possible
1/2 cup superfine sugar
1/4 cup candied fruit, citron or
    orange peel, finely chopped
1/4 cup semi-sweet chocolate,
    finely diced
1 teaspoon vanilla extract or
    1 teaspoon orange flavoring
1/4 cup chopped pistachio nuts,
    optional
powdered sugar

Dough: Sift the flour and salt into a bowl, make a well in the center and add the wine and sugar. Work the flour into the center until you have a firm dough, something like a noodle dough. If it is too crumbly add more wine. Do not let it become too sticky. Form it into a ball; wrap in a clean, slightly damp cloth and let rest for 2 hours. Place the dough on a lightly floured pastry cloth or board, and roll it out very thin, about 1/16 inch thick. Cut into 5-inch squares. Place the squares diamond-fashion, pointing toward you. Fold the ends over the pipe and seal the ends with a bit of water by pressing. Preheat the oil to 375° and fry the *cannoli* a few at a time until they are golden brown. Remove tubes; tongs are best for this as the rolls are fragile. Place the delicate pastries to drain on absorbent paper. Cool and fill with ricotta filling. Makes 12.

Filling: Press the ricotta through a sieve into a bowl. Beat it with an electric mixer until creamy and smooth. Add the sugar and beat until it is dissolved. Beat in the fruit, chocolate, and vanilla or orange flavoring. Place the filling into a pastry bag fitted with a large plain tube and pipe the filling into the cooled shells. Dip the filled shells into pistachio nuts and sprinkle with powdered sugar.

147

Nut Roll
Povitica

Rene Pagliai

Filling:
2 eggs
3 cups ground black walnuts
1/2 cup honey
2 tablespoons butter, melted
1 tablespoon cinnamon
1 teaspoon vanilla

Dough:
2 packages dry yeast
1/2 cup warm water
1/2 cup sugar, divided
1 cup sour cream
1/2 cup oleo, melted
2 eggs, beaten
4 cups flour

Filling: Combine all the ingredients and mix well.
Dough: Dissolve the yeast in warm water with 1 tablespoon sugar. Heat the sour cream. Remove from the heat, add the remaining sugar, oleo, and yeast mixture. Add the eggs and flour. Beat until it leaves the sides of the bowl. Refrigerate overnight or up to a week, covered. Divide the dough into thirds, and let rise until doubled in bulk. Roll out to a 14x10-inch rectangle. Divide the filling into thirds, spread one third on each dough rectangle and roll as you would for a jelly roll. Let rise until doubled in bulk. Bake at 350° for 25 to 30 minutes, or until browned. When done cover with a tea towel to cool. Makes about 3 dozen.

Mary Spallitta, left, and Florence Walsh hold bocci balls at Villa Scalbrini, Northlake, Illinois where they are volunteers at the home for the aged.

Siena Fruitcake
Panforte di Siena

Mary Spallitta

1/2 cup sifted cake flour
3 tablespoons cocoa
1 teaspoon cinnamon
1/2 teaspoon ground allspice
1/2 teaspoon ground nutmeg
1/2 cup honey
1/2 cup sugar
1/4 pound almonds, blanched, coarsely chopped
1/4 pound candied fruit, finely chopped
1/2 cup finely chopped candied lemon and orange peel
confectioner's sugar

Sift the flour with the cocoa and spices 3 times. In a saucepan heat the honey and sugar to boiling and boil 3 minutes, stirring constantly, over medium heat. Remove from the heat and quickly stir in the nuts, fruits, and dry ingredients. Immediately pour into a well-greased, 9-inch square pan which has been lined with waxed paper. Bake at 300° for 30 minutes or until the cake shrinks from the sides of the pan. Remove from the pan and peel off the waxed paper. Cool on a rack and sprinkle generously with confectioner's sugar. Store in an airtight container.

148

Honey Clusters
Pignolata

Sabina LoCurto

1 cup cake flour
1/2 cup butter, softened
7 cups all-purpose flour
8 large eggs
1/4 cup plus 2 tablespoons sugar, divided
1 to 2 tablespoons brandy, rum, or whiskey
peanut oil or vegetable oil for frying
1 to 1 1/2 pounds honey
rind of one large orange, grated
1 cinnamon stick, pulverized in a blender or 1 teaspoon ground cinnamon, optional
1 pound each walnuts and almonds, toasted and chopped
powdered sugar
colored candy confetti

Cut the butter into the cake flour. Put the all-purpose flour on a board and make a well in the center. Break the eggs into the well, add the cake flour mixture, 1/4 cup sugar, and your choice of liquor. Knead all the ingredients together quickly, leaving the dough as soft as possible.

Keeping dough covered with a bowl, cut off pieces of the dough. Roll each piece of the dough into a long cylinder about 1/4 inch in diameter. Cut into 1/4-inch pieces and place on a floured baking sheet. To prevent sticking during rolling and cutting, place cookie sheet in freezer periodically. Repeat until all the dough is used up. Place the pieces of dough in the freezer before frying.

To cook, heat 1 to 2 inches of oil in a saucepan. When hot, drop enough pieces to form a single layer into the oil and fry until lightly golden, not brown, about 1 to 2 minutes. Remove with a slotted spoon onto paper towels to absorb the excess oil. Repeat with the rest of the dough, controlling the temperature of the oil so the balls will not burn.

The balls may be finished at this time or set aside in a cool place to finish the next day. In a large pan, heat 1 pound honey with 2 tablespoons of sugar, orange rind, and cinnamon. Do not burn. When heated, add the nuts and balls of pastry. Stir until they are well coated with honey. If balls seem dry, add more honey. The honey should not drip. Prepare large platters by rinsing with cold water and sprinkling with sugar. This recipe will make several rings of different sizes or 1 large ring and some cones or clusters. Individual servings can be made by shaping 2 tablespoons of small balls into a cluster and placing them in cupcake liners for gift giving at holiday time. Keep your hands wet to prevent sticking, but work quickly. Press the shapes together so that the balls will adhere firmly. They may be sprinkled with powdered sugar or colored candy confetti. Cool. This will keep about a month in a metal container or about 6 months frozen.

Note: This recipe is Sicilian, and is used for Christmas. It is called *Strufoli* in Naples and *Cicirchiata* in Abruzzi where it is used for Mardi Gras.

Pizzelle
Waffle Cookies

Anna Pitzo
Glendale, Wisconsin
and
Rosalia Ferrante
Milwaukee, Wisconsin

Pizzelle *originated in the province of Abruzzi, Italy, a region east of Rome. They are dry and crisp; therefore they can be stored for an extended period of time in an airtight container. These thin, wafflelike cookies are versatile in their use. They can be eaten plain or used as sandwich cookies filled with one of the fillings listed below.*

Pizzelle *are not difficult to make but once were time-consuming to cook. A heavy cast iron waffle-type machine with long handles had to be held over a fire in the hearth and turned to cook each side of the cookie. This was usually done by the women of the household. It came to be a traditional holiday treat and also a cookie for other festive occasions such as weddings, baptisms, and first communions.*

Today we use the electric pizzelle *iron which is quick and easy to handle.*

6 eggs
1 1/2 cups sugar
1 cup margarine, (1/2 pound), melted
1 teaspoon anise oil
3 cups flour
2 teaspoons baking powder

Beat the eggs, adding the sugar gradually. Beat until smooth. Add the cooled melted margarine and anise oil. Sift the flour and baking powder and add to the egg mixture. The dough will be sticky enough to drop by a spoon. To make cookies follow the directions given with the *pizzelle* iron.

Note: The thickness of the pizzelle can be controlled by the texture of the dough. The thinner the dough, the thinner the cookie. If the pizzelles are to be used as sandwich cookies, a thicker dough is prepared by increasing the amount of flour by 1/2 cup.

Grape Filling:
1 cup chopped walnuts
1 cup grape jelly
1/4 cup Marsala or brandy
1 cup dates, cooked and chopped
1/2 cup raisins

Combine and let stand overnight.

Ceci Filling (Garbanzo Beans):
3 cans ceci (garbanzo beans), drained and ground
1/2 cup sugar
1 lemon rind, grated
1 cup honey
1 square chocolate
1/2 cup ground nuts

Place in a kettle over a low flame. Cook for one hour, stirring occasionally. Remove from heat and cool.

Right: Mary Balistreri Smith and Rosalia Ferrante demonstrate the old-fashioned way to make pizzelles at the Milwaukee, Wisconsin Holiday Folk Fair.

St. Joseph's Day Cream Puffs

Sfinge di San Giuseppe

Sabina LoCurto

1 tablespoon shortening
1 cup water
1 cup sifted flour
dash cinnamon
2 teaspoons baking powder
1/4 teaspoon salt
1 teaspoon grated orange rind
4 eggs
honey
powdered sugar
oil for frying

Optional Ricotta Filling:

1 pound ricotta cheese, drained
   overnight to remove
   excess water
2 tablespoons grated semi-sweet
   chocolate
1 tablespoon grated orange rind
2 teaspoons almond extract
sugar to taste

Place the water and shortening in saucepan. Bring to a boil. Add the flour, cinnamon, baking powder, salt, and orange rind, stirring vigorously until the mixture leaves the sides of the pan and forms a ball in the center of the pan. Cool to luke-warm. Add the eggs one at a time, beating vigorously after each until the mixture is smooth. Heat several inches of oil in a deep pan and drop the dough by spoonfuls into hot oil. Fry until puffed and golden, turning constantly, about 5 to 10 minutes. Drain on paper towels and cool. When cool drizzle with warmed honey and sprinkle with powdered sugar. This is a traditional Christmas pastry. For St. Joseph's Day, March 19, these puffs are filled with ricotta filling. Makes 12 to 18.

Ricotta Filling: Blend all the ingredients thoroughly. If too thick, add a few tablespoons of milk to make a smooth custard-like mixture. Keep chilled until ready to fill the puffs. To fill, split the puffs in half vertically, fill and press together. Set half of a maraschino cherry on top or in the center and sprinkle with powdered sugar.

Sal Anthony's Cheesecake
Torta di Ricotta alla Sal Anthony

Sal Anthony's
New York City

Italians base their cheesecake on whole milk ricotta and eggs. Apart from being lower in calories than its New York-style counterpart, a properly made Italian cheesecake has a lighter, fresher, more "dairy" flavor. This characteristic taste depends almost entirely on the freshness of the ricotta and the treatment you give it. It's best to go to an Italian cheese store where turnover is high and freshness almost assured. Once you have the ricotta, keep it tightly wrapped. When incorporating the ricotta with other ingredients, treat it gently in order not to break down the curds. For this reason I recommend using your hands.

8 eggs
1 cup granulated sugar
1 tablespoon anisette liqueur, optional
3 pounds whole milk ricotta cheese

Preheat the oven to 325°. Butter a 9-inch, high-sided round cake pan. Set aside. Break the eggs into a mixing bowl. Slowly add the sugar, mixing until the sugar is dissolved in the eggs. Do not whip air into the mixture. Add the anisette and stir. Add the ricotta to the bowl and mix well by hand. Do not use a machine. Pour the mixture into the cake pan. Place the pan in the oven for about 1 hour or until top of the cake turns golden brown. Do not overcook. Remove from the oven and let stand on a rack for 1 hour. Place in the refrigerator overnight. To serve, remove the cake from the refrigerator. Heat the bottom of the pan over the stove burner, turning the pan clockwise and counterclockwise vigorously until the cake loosens. Remove from the burner. Place a large plate over the cake pan and invert. Remove any excess liquid with paper towels. Place a serving tray on top of the cake; invert again. Refrigerate. The cake should be removed from the refrigerator 1 hour before serving. Sprinkle with powdered sugar.

Ricotta Cheesecake
Torta di Ricotta

Isabella Gardaphe
Melrose Park, Illinois

1 pound ricotta cheese
2 cups sour cream
2 packages (8-ounce) cream cheese, softened
1 1/2 cups sugar
1/2 cup melted butter
3 jumbo eggs
3 tablespoons flour
3 tablespoons cornstarch
5 teaspoons vanilla
5 teaspoons lemon juice

Preheat the oven to 350°. Beat the ricotta and sour cream together. Add the cream cheese, sugar, and butter; continue beating. Add the eggs, flour, cornstarch, vanilla, and lemon juice. Beat on the highest speed for 5 minutes. Pour into a 10-inch springform pan. Bake at 350° for 1 hour. Turn off the oven. Leave the cheesecake in with the oven door closed for one more hour. Cool on rack.

Wine Cookies
Biscotti

Rene Pagliai

1 stick butter
3/4 cup sugar
3 eggs
2 teaspoons baking powder
1 ounce anise extract or
   1 tablespoon crushed anise seed
2 1/2 to 3 cups flour
1/2 cup walnuts or almonds
powdered sugar

Cream the butter and sugar. Add the eggs one at a time. Add the baking powder, anise and flour, and mix well. Mix in the nuts. Divide the dough into thirds and form into rolls about the length of a cookie sheet. Flatten the tops so each roll is about 1 inch thick. Bake at 325° for 20 minutes. Cut the logs on an angle into 1-inch slices. Turn the slices on side and broil one side until browned, then the other side. Dust with powdered sugar.
   Biscotti means twice cooked.
Note: Biscotti are often dipped in wine when eaten.

Below: New York City, New York.
Photograph by Renato Rotolo.

Italian Fig Bars
Paste di Fichi

Mrs. Mary Onesi
Niagara Falls, New York

Mary and Paul Onesi had been married 71 years in 1988. Paul was born in Marco, Italy, and came to the United States to work in the coal mines of Pennsylvania. He had an arranged marriage with Mary, who was married at 14 years. This is her recipe for the traditional three-day fig cookie.

Filling:
1 pound figs, ground
1 pound dates, ground
2 cups raisins, ground
2 oranges, ground
2 cups walnuts, ground
1 teaspoon nutmeg
1 small can crushed pineapple
1 (8 ounce) jar strawberry jam

Pastry:
2 cups sugar
8 cups flour
7 teaspoons baking powder
1 teaspoon baking soda
2 cups shortening, melted
1 cup milk
6 eggs, beaten
1 tablespoon vanilla

Filling: Mix all the ingredients together. Set aside for 3 days.
Pastry: Mix the dry ingredients together. Add the liquid ingredients to make a dough. Roll the dough on a floured surface until it is pastry-thin. Cut into strips 3 inches wide. Place teaspoons of filling along the strips and then fold the pastry over the top. Cut the strips into 1 1/2-inch pieces. Bake at 350° for 12 to 15 minutes.

Egg Biscuits
Taralli

Maria Carmela Bartucci
Norridge, Illinois

Mrs. Bartucci, born in 1905, came to America with her husband, daughter and three sons after World War II. They farmed in Calabria, Italy. On the title page, she is pictured making biscuits and bread.

6 whole eggs, beaten
1/4 cup corn oil
1/2 teaspoon dry yeast
1 pound taralli flour (if not
    available substitute
    unbleached all-purpose flour)
1 tablespoon sugar, optional

Add the oil to the eggs. Mix in the yeast. Next add the flour, then the sugar, mixing well. This mixture will be very pasty to knead properly, so grease your hands. Knead well. When smooth, roll out a small ball (about 1-inch in diameter) into a long breadstick-like form. Bring the ends together and press to close. Meanwhile, boil water in a 4-quart pot. As the water slowly boils add the rings one or two at a time as the pot accommodates. When they've risen to the top, turn over for a few seconds, then remove to a dry cloth. Continue until all are boiled. Preheat the oven to 350°. Place each ring on a baking sheet on the middle rack of the oven and bake for about 10 minutes. Then check the color. If still light, bake for an additional 5 minutes. If browned, turn over for a minute or two until done. May be served as is or topped with icing.

Pine Nut Macaroons
Amaretti

Dolores Carlo
Coralville, Iowa

14 ounces almond paste
1 cup granulated sugar
1/2 teaspoon vanilla
1/8 teaspoon cinnamon
3 large egg whites
3/4 cup pine nuts, or more to taste
1/3 cup powdered sugar

With an electric mixer, cream together the almond paste and sugar. Add the vanilla, cinnamon, and egg whites, a little at a time, beating after each addition. Beat until smooth. Line baking sheets with baking or waxed paper. Drop the batter by teaspoons onto baking sheets, 1 inch apart. Stud each macaroon with pine nuts. Sift the powdered sugar over each and bake in a 300° oven 15 to 18 minutes or until pale golden. Transfer the macaroons to a rack to cool. Store in an airtight container, separated by waxed paper. Makes 70 cookies.

Sweet Ricotta Pie
Pizza Dolce

Rose Grieco
Montclair, New Jersey

Rose is the founder of Montclair's Italian Folklore Group.

Pie Crust:
1 cup flour, sifted
2/3 cup confectioner's sugar, sifted
1 tablespoon baking powder
1 stick butter, softened
3 egg yolks

Pie Filling:
1 1/2 pounds ricotta
1/2 cup sugar
3 egg whites
rind of 1 orange
2 tablespoons fresh orange juice

Pie Crust: Sift together the flour, sugar, and baking powder. Cut in the butter until the mixture resembles corn meal. Mix in the yolks and refrigerate for 15 minutes.
Pie Filling: Combine all the ingredients and mix well.
Assembly: Roll out the crust to fill an 8-inch pie tin. Roll out the leftover crust dough and cut it into strips for the top of pie. Place the filling in the crust and place the strips of dough cross-wise over the top. Bake at 300° for 1 hour. This can be made ahead of time and refrigerated until ready to bake.

Opposite: Wooden yard shrine crafted by furniture repairman Salvatore Borgia. Carroll Gardens, Brooklyn, New York.
Photograph by © Joseph Sciorra, 1987.

Gino's Tiramisu
Gino's "Pick Me Up" Cream Dessert

Gino Bartucci

sugar
9 large eggs, separated
500 grams mascarpone or
    8 ounces cream cheese,
    whipped and 8 ounces sour
    cream
12 cups brewed espresso
liqueur, your choice; most light
    sweet ones work well although
    orange-flavored liqueur is part
    of the original recipe
1 to 2 packages ladyfingers
grated baker's chocolate and/or
    grated orange rind

Beat 9 tablespoons of sugar into the the egg yolks. Blend in the mascarpone, and beat to a creamy texture. In another bowl, beat the egg whites until stiff; then fold into the yolk/cheese cream. Set aside. Sweeten the espresso to taste. Add the liqueur to taste. Moisten the ladyfingers one by one in the mixture and form a bottom layer in a trifle bowl. Now add a layer of the prepared cream. Next, you may sprinkle some of the grated chocolate and/or orange rind. Repeat the layers, ending with the cream and sprinkles of your choice. Can be served immediately, or must be refrigerated if prepared ahead. Spoon out to serve. Can also be cut into squares, provided that your cream has set. Another variation is to form as a torte in a cake pan. This can be done by creating a thicker, more set cream, and by not soaking the ladyfingers too long. Refrigerated, it can be kept up to a week without spoilage.

Too Toos
Chocolate Cookies

Mary Ann Maglio
Milwaukee, Wisconsin

5 cups flour
5 teaspoons baking powder
1/4 teaspoon cinnamon
1/2 cup cocoa
2 cups sugar
2 sticks butter
4 eggs, beaten
2 tablespoons orange juice
2 tablespoons lemon juice

Put the flour, baking powder, cinnamon, cocoa and sugar into a bowl. Cut in the butter and mix with your fingers until the mixture resembles corn meal. Add the remaining ingredients and mix well. Take small portions and form balls. Place on cookie sheet and bake at 350° for about 12 minutes or until golden. You may add chopped walnuts or peanuts to the dough.

Queen's Biscuits
Biscotti di Regina

Josephine Scalissi Grunewald

3 pounds flour
12 eggs
1 pound vegetable shortening
   or butter
6 teaspoons baking powder
1 1/2 pounds sugar
2 tablespoons vanilla
1 cup milk
1 egg
sesame seeds

Mix all but the last two ingredients. Roll out in thick ropes about 1 inch thick. Cut into 3-inch lengths and dip into the beaten egg, then the sesame seeds. Bake on greased sheets at 325° to 350° watching carefully to avoid burning. Remove when golden.

Anise Slices
Biscotti con Anisetta

Josephine Scalissi Grunewald

6 eggs, divided
1/2 teaspoon salt
1/2 cup sugar
4 cups flour
1 teaspoon baking powder
6 drops of anise oil (can be
   purchased at a drug store)
1 cup butter or shortening, softened
sugar for sprinkling

Beat 5 eggs with salt. Add the sugar and blend thoroughly. Sift the flour and baking powder together. Add to the egg mixture. Add the anise oil and shortening, and mix well. Knead until the dough is smooth and manageable. Roll the dough into an oblong loaf 5 inches wide by 3/4 inch thick. Brush with one beaten egg. Sprinkle with the sugar and cut into 1-inch slices. Place the slices in a greased baking dish and bake at 350° for 15 minutes or until light brown. Makes 2 1/2 dozen slices.

"Amici di tutti, amici di nessuno."
"A friend to all is a friend to none."
—*Judge Peter R. Scalise*
Chicago, Illinois

About the Editor

Fred L. Gardaphe is a Professor of English at Columbia College in Chicago. His play, *Vinegar and Oil,* was produced by the Italian American Theater Company in 1987. He is currently working on a Ph.D. in American Literature at the University of Illinois, Chicago, concentrating on Italian-American literature. He lives in Chicago with his wife Susan and their children, Frederico and Marianna.

Acknowledgments

Special thanks to Anthony Sorrentino of Hinsdale, Illinois, for his valued help in the planning and editing of this book. He is a founder and former Executive Director of the Joint Civic Committee of Italian Americans. In 1954 he received Italy's Star of Solidarity Award, and in 1983 the title *Cavaliere Ufficiale, Ordine al Merito.*

Ann (Mrs. Anthony) Sorrentino, food editor of *Fra Noi,* the Italian-American newspaper of the Chicago area, served as editor of the recipe section of this book.

We thank those who submitted recipes, and the many contributors to this book. They include Joseph and Sabina LoCurto; Barbara Collins; Joseph Maselli, president, American Italian Federation, New Orleans; Amie Giannone Stern, *Fra Noi,* North Lake, Illinois; John Lofgren, director, and Barbara Noel, volunteer, Sonoma County Museum, Jeannette Mitchell, North Bay Cultural Foundation, and Harold A. Lapham, all of Santa Rosa, California; Sarah R. Lea; Mr. and Mrs. Gino Bartucci; Anthony Bartucci; Sister Innocent Migliore, Mother Cabrini Shrine, Golden, Colorado; Armida Renada; Jacqueline Prato; Jennifer Quattrocchi; Lauri Jones; Mary Jane Puccio; Kerri Jones; the North End Italian Community Band of Boston, Massachusetts; Ruth Julin; Mary Ann Zug; Diane Heusinkveld, drawing, page 113; Maybelle Mays; Jane Viemeister; Dolores Fasano Olson; Georgia Heald; Kathryn Chadima; the Iowa City Public Library reference researchers; and many others.

Credits

Photography by Joan Liffring-Zug.

Graphic Design: Esther Feske and Judy Waterman.

Contributing editors and writers: Julie McDonald, Miriam Canter, Harry Oster, Michelle Nagle Spencer, Joan Liffring-Zug, and John Zug, Penfield Press.

Cover photo: *Adriana Bartucci in her grandmother's grape arbor in Norridge, Illinois.*

Back cover: *Anna Cesario is holding a seafood salad at Gino's Italian Imports in Chicago, Illinois. The dessert pictured is* cannoli.